WEAPON

THE CROSSBOW

MIKE LOADES

Series Editor Martin Pegler

OSPREY
Bloomsbury Publishing Plc
PO Box 883, Oxford, OX1 9PL, UK
1385 Broadway, 5th Floor, New York, NY 10018, USA
E-mail: info@ospreypublishing.com
www.ospreypublishing.com

OSPREY is a trademark of Osprey Publishing Ltd

First published in Great Britain in 2018

© Osprey Publishing Ltd, 2018

A catalogue record for this book is available from the British
Library.

ISBN: PB 9781472824608; eBook 9781472824622;
ePDF 9781472824615; XML 9781472824639

18 19 20 21 22   10 9 8 7 6 5 4 3 2 1

Index by Rob Munro
Typeset by PDQ Digital Media Solutions, Bungay, UK
Printed in China through World Print Ltd.

Osprey Publishing supports the Woodland Trust, the UK's
leading woodland conservation charity. Between 2014 and 2018
our donations are being spent on their Centenary Woods project
in the UK.

To find out more about our authors and books visit **www.
ospreypublishing.com**. Here you will find extracts, author
interviews, details of forthcoming events and the option to sign
up for our newsletter.

Cover (above): Crossbow (A1032) *c.*1487–1500. Steel lath,
covered with parchment; tiller of carved antler. A painted coat-
of-arms identifies this crossbow as having once belonged to the
Völs Colonna family, from the South Tyrol. (© The Wallace
Collection, London)
Cover (below): © Osprey Publishing.
Title-page photograph: A 14th-century image of two men with
crossbows. One man is spanning his bow by lifting his leg to
push down on the stirrup. The other holds his crossbow at
shoulder height to shoot it. Both crossbows have
characteristically long tillers and the laths have a knobbly
appearance, suggesting that they are wooden with the knots left
proud by the bowyer. Royal 2 B. VII, f.162v: image taken from
the *Queen Mary Psalter*, *c.*1310–20. (British Library (CC0 1.0))

Dedication
For Tobias Capwell

Author's acknowledgements
I owe a particular debt of gratitude to my friend David Joseph
Wright, who has not only provided me with many splendid line
drawings to illustrate the text but has been also a constant
sounding-board throughout the writing process. Leo Todeschini
of Tod's Stuff and Andreas Bichler have also made singular
contributions. Both of these gentlemen have provided me with
wonderful photographs of the magnificent replicas that they have
made and also shared with me their deep knowledge of the
subject in patient correspondence. Similarly, I have plundered the
brains of a long list of friends, much brighter than I. Among
them are Tobias Capwell, John Waller, Lukas Novotny, Chris
Boyton, Hector Cole MBE, Ralph Moffat, Alan Williams, Mark
Hatch, Peter Dekker, Justin Ma and Stephen Selby. I thank them
all. As ever I am enormously grateful to my wife Kim Hawkins,
for her support and encouragement, as well as for her superb
photography.

Editor's note
For the most part, measurements are given using the imperial
scale. Exceptions are made for energy and force, for which metric
units such as the joule (J) and the newton (N) are used. The
following data will help when converting between imperial and
metric measurements:

1 mile = 1.6km
1 yard = 0.9m
1 foot = 0.3m
1 inch = 25.4mm
1lb = 0.45kg
1J = 0.74 foot-pound force
1N = 0.22 pound-force

Artist's note
Readers may care to note that the original paintings from which
the colour plates in this book were prepared are available for
private sale. All reproduction copyright whatsoever is retained by
the publishers. All enquiries should be addressed to:

Peter Dennis, 'Fieldhead', The Park, Mansfield, Nottinghamshire
NG18 2AT, UK, or email magie.h@ntlworld.com

The publishers regret that they can enter into no correspondence
upon this matter.

CONTENTS

INTRODUCTION

The crossbow has long enjoyed a popular cachet for dastardly cunning and villainy. It was the subject of two papal bans (in 1096 and in 1139). These incurred a penalty of excommunication, excepting for its use against infidels. Anna Komnene, the Byzantine princess who left an eyewitness account of the First Crusade (1095–99), concluded that the crossbow was a diabolical mechanism, describing it as 'verily a devilish invention' (Komnene 2009: 282). In England a national love-affair with the longbow, enduring to the present day, has tended to eclipse the military importance of the crossbow in the popular imagination.

A trilogy of crossbow attacks on English kings in the 12th century further feed an unwarranted notion that it is somehow an underhand weapon. While hunting in the New Forest, William II Rufus (r. 1087–1100) was killed by a crossbow bolt; an assassin's blow conferring an association of perfidy to the weapon. His son Henry I (r. 1100–35) narrowly escaped a bolt shot by his illegitimate daughter Juliana in her failed attempt at both patricide and regicide. In 1199, in France, the English king Richard I (r. 1189–99) died as a result of gangrene, occasioned by a crossbow bolt in the shoulder at the siege of Châlus Castle. The sniper, famously equipped with a lowly frying-pan as a shield, was a commoner by the name of Peter Basilius. His action, carrying the apparent stain of being unchivalrous, was another blemish on the reputation of the crossbow.

Such a legacy is undeserved. Chivalry was a code of behaviour among nobles of equal status – it did not extend to other ranks, nor did it restrict the use of the most capable weapons for the combat at hand. The papal bans were never taken very seriously, intended as they were to curtail the endemic internecine violence among fellow European knights, rather than to ostracize the crossbow itself. Crossbows were ever a high-status hunting arm for the nobility and remained prestigious weapons in general use throughout the medieval period.

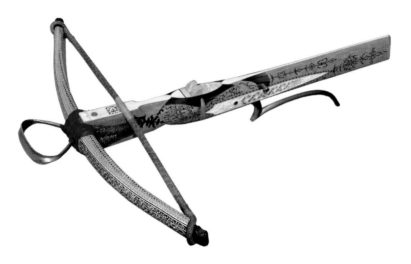

Although not new to history, the crossbow had been absent from the European battlefield until its appearance at the end of the 10th century. A few were suspicious of these seemingly new-fangled contraptions, but reactionary voices were quickly drowned out by the louder clamour for military advantage. Prior to the longbow's dominance in 14th-century English armies, the crossbow was considered by far the more useful weapon. Moreover, both in continental Europe and in England, the crossbow was the weapon of choice for defending castles and fortified towns from the late 11th to the mid-15th centuries. After that the ubiquity of the crossbow began to fade, increasingly obscured behind a pall of gunpowder.

An abiding modern perception is that the crossbow is a weapon of superior technological sophistication and of greater power than the longbow. Though it undoubtedly incorporated some mechanical ingenuity, attributions to its power have been overstated. Very powerful, steel-lathed crossbows did evolve in the 15th century, but during the time of its greatest supremacy on the battlefield – roughly from 1100 to 1250 – the crossbow packed a more modest punch. Its martial merits hinged not on its power, but on other factors. These included ease of use, comparatively inexpensive ammunition and the ability to hold a bow at full span for a sustained period, waiting to seize the optimal moment for a shot. This latter element was of particular benefit in siege warfare, both for attack and defence, and also at sea. For the hunter, too, the crossbow's chief advantage was that it could remain spanned and ready to shoot. It offered stillness and imperceptible movement at the moment of shooting, reducing the risk of startling an animal before the bolt struck home.

This study focuses primarily on the military crossbow of the European Middle Ages and Renaissance, though I have also presented what I consider to be necessary historical and global context with the inclusion of a few crossbows from the Ancient World. In introducing the European crossbow, there is an inevitable English bias to much of the discussion, partly because this undertaking is in English and partly because the crossbow in English armies has been too often neglected in favour of its more féted cousin, the longbow. There is a need to redress that balance.

In a work of this size, it is impossible to also cover the many other variants of the crossbow that occur in places such as Africa, Japan and South-East Asia. Nor is it possible to examine the equally interesting stonebow – a variant of the crossbow that featured a double string with a pouch. This propelled either a stone or a clay pellet, used primarily for shooting birds.

Even after they were obsolete on the battlefield, crossbows continued to develop with improved locks, differently shaped stocks and powerful laths. Hunting crossbows and target crossbows remained popular throughout the 16th, 17th and 18th centuries. These are the crossbows that mostly populate our national museums. They include glorious specimens, fine works of art; princely arms of the highest order. However, these were not the soldier's weapon. That has left a more ghostly mark, to be glimpsed at only in the dusty pages of inventories and ordnances and with faint glimmers in manuscript art. It is that weapon which is the primary concern in the brief survey that follows.

Terminology

It is necessary at times to distinguish between regular hand-held bows and crossbows. The Close Rolls of Edward II (CCR Ed II) include several references to the term **hand-bow** in order to make the distinction, as do documents as late as the 17th century. I shall follow that practice here and also use the term **regular** to indicate hand-bows as opposed to crossbows.

An **arbalist** is an alternative name for a crossbowman or, sometimes, a crossbow-maker. When spelled 'arbalest', some dictionaries assign the meaning to be the crossbow itself. The distinction is one of little difference, since both are derived from erratic medieval spelling and the intended meaning is best gauged from context.

Arrow, **bolt** and **quarrel** are all commonly used terms for the projectile, though 'quarrel' is specific to a type of military bolt fitted with a distinctive octahedron head.

The attachment of the lath to the tiller was by means of a cord or leather binding known as a **bridle**. The term 'bridle' may also be used to describe the cord loop fastened to a cranequin.

Also known as a **rack** or a **cric**, a **cranequin** is a spanning device whereby the turning handle operates on a ratchet bar via toothed gear wheels.

A **false string** is a bowstring that is longer than the correctly fitting string proper. It fits, without strain, onto a second set of nocks at the terminals of the limbs, enabling them to be bent sufficiently to allow the string proper to be put in place. It is more widely known today as a **bastard string**, but 'false string' is the idiom used in medieval documents.

Lath refers to the bow of a crossbow. During the last century the word **prod** entered everyday speech as an alternative term. As W.F. Paterson explains, however, this usage originated from a 19th-century mistranscription of the word *rodd* in a list of crossbow effects from an inventory of Henry VIII's possessions in 1547 (Paterson 1990: 28). Paterson recommends that the only correct terms are either lath or bow. I shall follow his guidance.

Lock is the name given to the release mechanism. This includes the catch for the string, sears, the trigger lever and the housing.

Power-stroke is the distance of string travel from the strung, resting position of the string to its location at full draw. The length of the lath has a direct bearing on how far the string can be retracted. The shorter the lath, the shorter the power-stroke and thus the less time and distance is available for the forces to act upon the projectile.

Spanning and **bending** are both terms for the action of pulling back the bowstring to full-draw.

Stock is the wooden stock onto which the bow is mounted. It is also known by the more common medieval name **tiller**. Either term is correct.

DEVELOPMENT
Lock, stock and lath

CROSSBOWS IN THE ANCIENT WORLD

Chinese crossbows

Archaeological finds of locks made from cast bronze announce the appearance of the crossbow in China around 650 BC, during the Spring and Autumn period (771–476 BC). Since crossbow locks may also be manufactured from organic materials – bone or wood – the crossbow may have existed prior to this period but, to date, there is no evidence for it.

The extent to which the string could be drawn back was a significant advantage in the design of the Chinese crossbow, compared to the European variety. A greater distance of string travel enabled more work to be done, so that more potential energy was stored in the bent bow. It also transferred energy to the arrow for longer – a longer barrel on a gun confers a similar benefit. It took around 20 inches to draw a Chinese crossbow string from its resting position to hook it behind the trigger

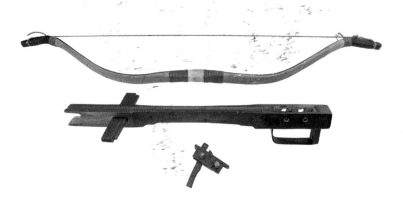

The disassembled parts of a Chinese crossbow – lock, stock and lath. Note that the composite lath has the shape and proportions of a regular hand-bow. In fact, in many cases, it was a normal hand-bow. Bows, perhaps captured from an enemy, which had in the past been shot by hand, could be pressed into service for use by relatively unskilled troops, simply by lashing them to wooden tillers fitted with mass-produced bronze locks. Two transverse wooden wedges provided a brace against which to tension the lashing cords. Converting hand-bows to crossbows necessarily produced crossbows of lower draw-weights, less than 150lb, which was towards the upper end for regular bows. Bows with a heavier draw-weight had to be specially made for the crossbow. With the longer power-stroke of the Chinese crossbow, however, even lower-weight bows offered a useful military performance, especially when used en masse. (Kim Hawkins)

Consisting of several moving parts, the lock of a Chinese crossbow had a short, vertical trigger lever, which could be operated by one or two fingers. This contrasted with the long, horizontal trigger lever required to release the rolling-nut on European crossbows. Once the workings were assembled, the lock housing was easily slotted into a recess in the tiller and secured with two bronze rods. This replica was built by Yang Fuxi. (Kim Hawkins)

catch. By contrast, on a European crossbow the power-stroke was typically only 4–5 inches. In part this longer power-stroke was made possible by the design of the Chinese lock, allowing it to locate at the tail-end of the tiller. The long horizontal lever on European crossbows necessitated placing the string-catch much further forward.

Longer power-strokes were also achievable owing to the style of bow. As early as the Warring States period (475–221 BC), it was common to arm the Chinese crossbow with a horn-and-sinew composite lath in the style of a standard recurve hand-bow. In fact, because the regular hand-bows of the period were relatively short, Chinese crossbows could be fitted with them without adaptation.

Once the workings were assembled, the lock housing was easily slotted into a recess in the tiller and secured with two bronze rods. Note the sighting-pin, which served double duty by also acting as a cocking-lever to reset the lock. Incised markings at the rear of the sighting-pin calibrated the elevation of the shot. (Kim Hawkins)

Compared to the shorter and stockier laths of European crossbows, these bows could be pulled back much further without fear of breaking. Similarly, a carriage-spring-style lath made from bamboo strips, also in common use, had a far longer limb-length/draw-length ratio than any European counterpart.

Early Chinese crossbows were spanned by sitting on the ground, bracing the feet against the bow and pulling the string back with both hands. Subsequently, during the Ming Dynasty (1365–1644) the crossbowman used a cord in the manner of a stirrup in order to span his weapon while standing. For the average recruit – a peasant on a low-protein diet – either spanning method probably limited the power of these bows to less than 250lb draw-weight and many were likely a good deal lighter than this, particularly since most were repurposed hand-bows. During the Han Dynasty (206 BC–AD 220), however, it was claimed that a few elite troops were capable of bending crossbows by the hands-and-feet method, with a draw-weight in excess of 750lb (Selby 2000: 172). This seems to stretch credulity not only for the power of the shooters, but also for the capacity of the lock. Whether or not a few men possessed such Herculean might we may never know. Nevertheless, the principle advantage of the crossbow was that it required little training and it could be used to equip tens of thousands of relatively low-grade troops. For reasons of stamina and to gain the advantages of rapid shooting, crossbows with lower draw-weights had a more broadly useful military application.

The discovery in 2015 of a nearly intact crossbow in pit 1 of the Terracotta Army at Xi'an, revealed a recurve composite lath measuring around 57 inches. A sizeable bow, it was found together with a pair of curved pieces of wood, each with three holes. These were *tepeliks* (see

An advantage that the Chinese crossbow enjoyed over its European counterpart was that the design of its lock permitted a significantly longer power-stroke. Chinese crossbows spanned approximately 26 inches from the front of the tiller to the nut, compared to approximately 10 inches for a European crossbow. European crossbows would require many times the amount of power in order to match performance. (Kim Hawkins)

9

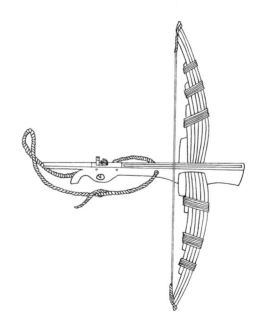

A far less expensive style of lath for the Chinese crossbow was made in the style of a carriage spring. It consisted of five strips of bamboo, steamed to shape, with each strip reduced in length incrementally. The shortest strip was on the belly of the bow, with the inside face towards the crossbowman. Hemp bindings at intervals along the limbs held it all together. Note also the cord passing through the stock just behind the lath, which served double duty. It was both a lanyard that enabled the crossbow to be carried over the shoulder on the march and also a proto-stirrup that allowed the bow to be hand-spanned with the crossbowman standing fully upright. (David Joseph Wright)

Loades 2016: 27) – wooden formers – that were tied to the bow to guard against any twist and to preserve the even curve of each limb during storage or travel, but removed for action. To date, 288 crossbow mechanisms have been excavated from pit 1. It is notable that these others were not complete with bows. Crossbow locks were mass-produced items, which were inexpensive and readily available. By contrast, the sinologist and practising archer Stephen Selby has calculated that it would have taken approximately 3,261 man-years of labour to equip all 1,087 terracotta crossbowmen with composite bows for their weapons (Selby 2000: 170).

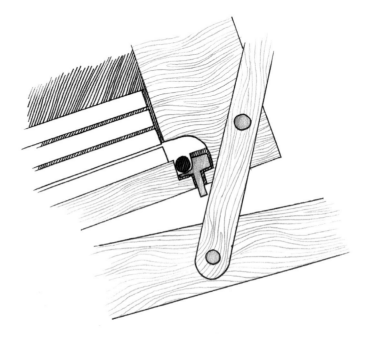

The key to the repeating crossbow being able to cycle shots is this T-shaped peg. It hangs freely in the string groove. When the string is engaged it drops down, allowing the string to locate. At the end of the lever pull, the magazine is brought flush with the stock, forcing the T-peg upwards and so pushing the string out of its groove to release the shot. (David Joseph Wright)

After the Qin Dynasty (221–206 BC), the crossbow remained in use in China but, in contrast to the development path of the European crossbow, it became less sophisticated, less expensive and much quicker to produce. Instead of using composite laths, the Chinese substituted multiple bamboo strips. Often these were weapons of lesser power, requiring poisoned arrows to make them effective.

The Chinese repeating crossbow – which transliterates from the Chinese as the *chu ko nu* – was capable of shooting successive bolts from a magazine by means of the continuous operation of a lever. It was, for the most part, a low-cost peasants' weapon, constructed using mulberry wood. Laths were sometimes also fashioned from mulberry and sometimes

Two views of an original Chinese repeating crossbow from the salerooms of Mandarin Mansion. It dates to the early 20th century, but its design remains unchanged since the earliest incarnations in the 3rd century BC. The double bamboo bow has a draw-weight estimated at above 70lb. At the forward cycle of the lever, the notch in the magazine housing engaged the string. As soon as the string went behind the notch, it created sufficient clearance for gravity to cause one of the unfletched bolts in the magazine to drop onto the bolt channel. When the lever was pulled back, both string and magazine were brought to full draw. During this cycle the tail-end of the magazine travels up and over in an arc, pivoting on transverse pins through the lever handle. There is a small, free-moving, T-shaped peg that hangs through a hole in the magazine beneath the string notch. When the lever is brought back fully, the magazine makes contact with the stock and this peg automatically pushes the string up, releasing it from the notch. The bolt is shot and the lever moves forward in a continuous cycle to reload. In operation, the T-bar at the end of the stock rests against the hip, the left hand holds beneath the stock, and the right hand shuttles the lever. (Images courtesy of Peter Dekker at Mandarin Mansion: Antique Arms and Armor)

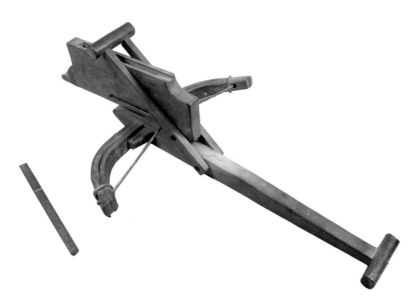

built with several strips of bamboo. These unglued strips were held in place by the bowstring, which passed through holes at each end of the lath. Wedges held the centre securely in the stock. Most magazines held ten bolts, though there are instances of larger types carrying 12 or 15 bolts. The *chu ko nu* varied in size. Some versions, equipped with twin magazines and twin bolt grooves, were able to shoot two darts simultaneously.

One tradition for the origin of the *chu ko nu* gives its name as the homophonic *zhuge nu* and claims that it was invented by the Chinese military strategist Zhuge Liang (AD 181–234). Even so, there is archaeological evidence for the *chu ko nu* as early as the late Warring States period and it may have existed even earlier than that.

In order to minimize the risk of a jam, bolts were not fletched, allowing them to sit in the magazine with parallel alignment. The absence of fletchings resulted in relatively erratic flight over distance, but the *chu ko nu* was not sufficiently powerful to perform well over great distances, and this was not its purpose. It was a short-range weapon that had the advantage of putting numbers of arrows into the air rapidly. In theory it could be shot as quickly as a person could move the handle to and fro. In practice, though, doing this leads not only to jams but to an extremely jerky action, in turn creating an erratic aim. It is essential to use smooth, rhythmic strokes that maintain the weapon in a relatively still position. The string was subject to a great deal of abrasion when in continuous use. For this reason it was reinforced with a finely sanded piece of split goose quill slotted over the centre section.

After shooting its initial salvos during the Warring States period, the *chu ko nu* seems to disappear from the record until the Ming Dynasty (1368–1644). A Chinese encyclopaedia from the Qing Dynasty (1644–1912), the *Guin Tushu Jicheng*, declares that, 'The Zhuge Nu is a handy little weapon that even the Confucian scholar [i.e. a weakling] or palace women can use in self-defence' (Peter Dekker 2017: private correspondence). This underlines its role as the 'home protection crossbow', by which name it was also known. The source goes on to state that, 'It fires weakly so you have to tip the darts with poison. Once the darts are tipped with "tiger-killing poison", you can shoot it at a horse or a man and as long as you draw blood, your adversary will die immediately. The draw-back to the weapon is its very limited range'. Whether used by peasants defending their village against marauding hordes of horsemen in the Warring States period or in urban guerrilla warfare as late as the Boxer Rebellion (1899–1901), tiger-killing poison, most probably compounded from aconite, gave the *chu ko nu* a lethal advantage. Repeating crossbows without poison darts were popular for harvesting wildfowl. When a skilled stalker could get close enough to a raft of ducks, these speedy weapons could be used to shoot at multiple targets as they took flight.

In addition to the lightweight hand-held types, much larger versions of the *chu ko nu* also appeared during the Ming Dynasty. These featured immensely powerful composite laths, often requiring a two-man crew to

A multiple-bolt, single-bow, siege crossbow. Mounted on a shooting table, this version has an immensely long lath that appears to be of composite, recurve construction. Some varieties, from at least the 2nd century BC, had the capacity to shoot several bolts at once. Multiple-shot crossbows had a broad stock with the relevant number of parallel bolt grooves; usually seven. Fanning out from the centre, each one was a few inches shorter than its neighbour. One account from AD 950 describes a 'rapid dragon engine', whereby several multiple-bolt crossbows were linked together with one central release (Turnbull 2001: 14). (Japan Archive Picture Library)

operate them. Shot from the ramparts of fortresses or the gunwales of ships, the larger weapons had to be mounted onto some form of support. Woodblock images from the Imjin War between Japan and Korea (1592–98) show the great *chu ko nu* being deployed at sea to rake the decks of an enemy ship prior to a boarding action.

Similar to the European 'great-crossbow' (see below), the Chinese deployed an outsize weapon of immense proportions. A text from the early 4th century BC, concerning the warlord Mo Zi, refers to crossbows built on a four-wheeled framework, standing 8 feet high and requiring a crew of ten men (Turnbull 2001: 13). Supposedly, the missiles for this colossus were 10 feet in length, projecting 3 feet in front of the stock, and were attached to a line so that they could be retrieved. We might surmise that there is some exaggeration in this account, but there can be no doubt that very large crossbows existed.

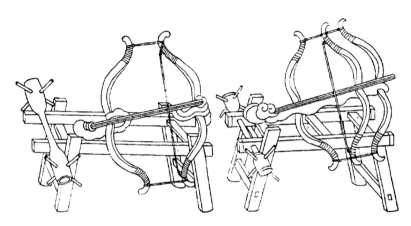

During the Song Dynasty (960–1279), both the double-lath (at far left) and the triple-lath crossbow (at left) made an appearance. All the laths are of stout, recurve, horn-and-sinew composite construction, with each acting upon the other by means of a continuous string that is secured at the end of the forward lath and then loops over the curled tips of the secondary (and tertiary) laths. Locks were proportionately larger versions of the standard lock in cast bronze used for the standard Chinese crossbow and both are spanned by means of a bench-mounted windlass. These immensely powerful artillery pieces had no equivalent in the Western world, though they did migrate to parts of South-East Asia, where they were used, mounted on the backs of elephants! (Japan Archive Picture Library)

A modern replica of a *gastraphetes* made by Leo Todeschini. The bow has been fabricated from modern materials, but it conforms to the shape and proportions suggested by Heron of Alexandria's drawing. In use, the slider is brought forward until the claw at the front of the trigger block engages the string. The front end of the slider is then braced against the ground. Note the two bronze strips of ratchet teeth positioned either side of the tiller. Once a significant strain was engaged, pawls attached to the trigger block engaged with these teeth to hold the tension. Thereby the string could be pushed back in gradual, controlled increments. (Photograph: Tod's Stuff)

Greek crossbows

The crossbow of the Ancient Greeks was an ingenious weapon that incorporated a slider mechanism to draw back the string. It was known as the *gastraphetes* (belly-shooter) because the shooter leant partially into the device with his belly in order to push the slider back. Heron of Alexandria documented the first surviving explanation of how the *gastraphetes* worked in the 1st century AD, following the now-lost record of Ctesibus in the 3rd century BC. It is a detailed account, including a drawing, which allows for reasonably accurate modern reconstruction. No other visual record occurs in Greek art. Opinion is divided regarding the date of the *gastraphetes*' invention, though it may have been as early as the 5th century BC.

Like the Chinese crossbow, the *gastraphetes* employed a full-size composite bow, made in the same style as the hand-bow of the time. It had an exceptionally long draw-length. Maximum draw-weights can only be estimated, but an upper limit of around 120lb seems probable. Other Greek and Roman artillery – *ballistae* and the like – mimicked the slider with a pawl-and-ratchet system. Although *ballistae* are frequently likened

Detail of the trigger block for a *gastraphetes*. Made from bronze, the block sits at the back end of the slider. Note that the claw has engaged the string and has been locked into place by a lever, which also acts as the trigger. Before the bow is spanned the pawls will be flipped to be forward-facing, so that they engage the ratchet teeth. (Photograph: The Hoplite Association)

to 'giant crossbows', it is incorrect to do so. They do not have bows but rather two separated and independent arms that are powered by twisted skeins of sinew; they operate with torsion power; a bow employs tension power.

Roman crossbows

To date, the only contemporary accounts of the *arcuballista* – the Roman crossbow – appear in the pages of *De Re Militaris*, written by Vegetius in the late 4th century AD. Drawing on a miscellany of earlier sources, Vegetius makes frustratingly vague references. He writes at one stage about crossbowmen lining up with other artillerymen (using torsion machines) in line of battle and at another about both *sagittarii* (regular archers)

and *arcuballistarii* (crossbowmen) working together on siege towers to clear the ramparts of defenders. These are flickering glimpses, however; he gives little indication of the extent to which the *arcuballista* was used in warfare, or of the numbers of troops in a legion who might have been armed with it.

Fortunately, two Gallo-Roman carved reliefs in France, at Salignac and Saint-Marcel, offer tantalizing glimpses of the form. In both cases it is clear that the crossbow is being carried in a hunting context. Consistent in both carvings are three elements: a composite lath, a square stock and a distinctive shape to the butt. It is also apparent from the Salignac example that the draw-length is longer than that of later medieval crossbows. It shot a longer arrow and both carvings show a quiver suitable for longer arrows. In this regard it was similar both to Chinese and to Greek antecedents and different from medieval crossbows. In practical trials, the positioning of the trigger, the shape of the handgrip and the balance of the weapon suggested that it was shot from the hip. It was most natural to shoot it in roughly the same position as it was held for spanning, making it quick and ergonomic to use.

Employing a replica made by Leo Todeschini, Steve Senior of The Hoplite Association demonstrates how the *gastraphetes* is spanned by leaning into it and pushing the slider against the ground. Bows of military power may need to be braced against a more solid surface in order to avoid the slider embedding. The rocky terrain of the Eastern Mediterranean would have provided adequate resistance, however. (Photograph: The Hoplite Association)

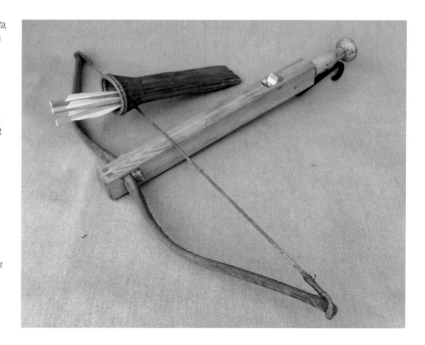

An interpretation of the *arcuballista*, built by Leo Todeschini. The length of the composite lath is around 39 inches and the string can be drawn back around 16 inches to engage with the nut, allowing 22-inch arrows to be shot. Although difficult to discern in this photograph, there is a shallow bolt groove running along the top of the tiller. The shape of the trigger lever is speculative, but the return curl at the end aids one-handed operation, which could make such a weapon suitable for horsemen. A composite lath would be very light and the shape of the handle suggests the possibility of one-handed use. The length of the lever is determined by the closeness of the nut to the tail-end of the tiller. To hold the lath in place, wedges have been used instead of a cord bridle and the front of the tiller has been reinforced with two ash pegs because the stresses would otherwise be too great. (Photograph: Tod's Stuff)

The release mechanism is not clear on the carvings, but it looks as if it may be a rolling-nut, as found on later crossbows. In 1893, archaeologists digging at Southgrove Farm (Burbage, Wiltshire) unearthed a rolling-nut made from bone. From the context of the find site it was dated to the Roman period. The invention of the rolling-nut was a breakthrough that had an immense impact on the development of the crossbow.

No mechanical spanning device is shown in the sculptural evidence, suggesting a bow of relatively light draw-weight. In tests with a replica, Leo Todeschini used a bow with a 45lb draw-weight. He experimented by placing the rounded end of the tiller against his lower stomach and drawing the string back with both hands. He found this to be both comfortable and efficient. With the 45lb bow he shot the 22-inch arrows a distance of over 100 yards. Such power may be adequate for hunting small game but of little military application. One idea, suggested by the dome at the base of the tiller, would be to have a thick, moulded-leather cup incorporated into a leather belt to aid spanning. Locating the dome into the cup would spread the load and prevent the tiller from slipping. With such a system, draw-weights in excess of 130lb may have been achievable.

A series of images showing a replica of a rolling-nut made from antler by Leo Todeschini. The claw of the nut is bifurcated creating two 'fingers'. The gap between these allows the insertion of the bolt so that its tail-end sits flush against the string. On the underside of the nut is a little notch into which the sear of the trigger catches, preventing rotation until the trigger is released. Note the little iron plate at the point of maximum friction, protecting the antler from wear and providing a smooth, hard surface for the trigger-sear both to hold against and to disengage from. (Photographs: Tod's Stuff)

THE EUROPEAN MEDIEVAL CROSSBOW

The lock

The challenge for a crossbow lock is to be able to overcome the friction generated by the taut string of a spanned bow pulling against it. The more powerful the bow; the greater the friction. Imagine a stout post embedded in the ground. A rope passes around the post and is held in tension at either end by two strong friends standing in front of the post and leaning back with all their might. Try to knock the rope up and off the post with your hand. Provided that your friends are strong enough, they should be able to generate sufficient friction against the post that you are unable to dislodge the rope. The ability to overcome these forces is determined by the design of the crossbow lock and trigger.

The vast majority of crossbows employed some form of rolling-nut as the release catch. These were mostly made of bone or antler, lightweight materials that spun with little inertia. Rolling-nuts sat in a precisely carved recess in the stock, known as a saddle. On release, the nut rotated freely within the saddle. When the string was engaged, the front of the nut pushed against the front of the saddle. A bone veneer lined the forward end of the saddle, strengthening it and reducing friction. There was no axle for the nut; tremendous forces were at work and a narrow axle would have bent. The centre hole did not provide the axis for spin, but rather facilitated a means for retaining the nut. In order to prevent the nut from jumping out at the moment of shooting or when being carried, a band of cords passed through the centre hole and bound around the outside of the tiller.

In the collections of the Metropolitan Museum of Art, New York are fragments of a rolling-nut that were excavated at Montfort Castle in Palestine and which date to before that castle's destruction in 1271. The nut was fashioned from staghorn and shows traces of iron reinforcement. There is considerable stress on the nut when the bow is spanned and some examples had a metal pin inserted into each finger of the claw to strengthen it. Most also had a plate of metal on the underside of the nut, where it engaged with the sear of the trigger.

Various, more complex, systems were developed during the 16th century and beyond for both target and hunting crossbows. These entailed a separate sear interacting between the trigger lever and the nut. Resetting them involved a short cord that hung outside the body of the tiller. Later, even more complex mechanisms made an appearance, some having two cords for setting multiple sears. Such intricate devices were not ideal for military service and are beyond the scope of this present work.

FAR LEFT Example of the 'rising peg' system. The drawn string hooked into a transverse slot in the stock of the crossbow and the trigger lever operated a wooden peg that pushed up from beneath the string to release it above the slot. A significant drawback is the limited ability of the rising peg to overcome powerful loads. It is therefore restricted to bows of relatively light draw-weight. Nevertheless, its simplicity and ease of manufacture made it a popular choice for poachers and for members of the mob at times of civil unrest. (David Joseph Wright)

LEFT The trigger for the early-medieval crossbow had the benefit of great simplicity. A Z-shaped lever engaged the nut directly. It pivoted on a pin, with the sear end considerably shorter than the longer lever end. The greater weight of the lever end tended to hold the sear end in place but for added security a horn, and later steel, spring was added. (David Joseph Wright)

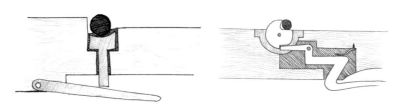

The tiller

In order to withstand the repeated strains of a powerful bow at full span, the tiller had to be tough. Single billets of wood were fashioned with gradual curves and robust proportions. Fruitwoods were popular choices, especially pear and cherry; hornbeam, hawthorn, walnut and maple also appear with regularity. As well as displaying attractive figure – that is the patterning on the finished surface – what these woods all have in common is the potential for interlocking grain. Interlocking grain occurs when spiral-grained trees alternate their annual direction of growth. It is highly resistant to splitting, obviously an advantage for a crossbow tiller, but it also makes the timber harder to work for the crossbow-maker. Most crossbows were also reinforced with an iron pin, set vertically through the front of the tiller.

The weapon historian Josef Alm quotes a reference in Burgundian accounts from 1384 to 'a complete crossbow in the Genoese fashion with iron bands' (Alm 1994: 25). He goes on to explain that these bands were for reinforcement of the stock on either side of the lock. Clearly, such buttressing suggests bows of enormous power. As a more decorative alternative to metal, the sides of the tiller, known as the cheeks, were often strengthened with plates of bone or antler.

While munition crossbows were mostly left plain, those made for wealthy patrons had highly decorated stocks. Full or partial veneers, using either cowhorn or staghorn, were common. Staghorn in particular lent itself to bold relief carving. Alternatively, either material could be used for elaborate inlay, often creating figurative scenes of great intricacy. Brass nails or brass bands might sometimes be added for additional opulent accent and colour was occasionally introduced with painted features. The crossbow could be both functional and a work of art. Even relatively unadorned specimens were given a veneer of polished bone or antler along the top of the tiller, where the string passed, so as to minimize friction. The lath was set into the tiller at an angle a little forward of 90 degrees to ensure the string did not abrade too much.

In the late-medieval period a notched ridge was fitted on top of the butt-end of some tillers. This enabled the shooter, whose fingers operated the trigger lever on the underside, to place his thumb in calibrated positions and to use his thumb knuckle as a sighting aid.

The length of tillers varied. To some extent this was determined by the spanning device. With a windlass, for instance, it was ergonomic for the centre of the winding handles to sit just above waist height; whereas with the cranequin the winding could be more easily managed with a shorter stock. Shorter stocks also offered easier portability and were especially convenient for the man on horseback.

Wooden laths

Despite the fact that composite-bow technology was in use during the Roman era and that there is evidence for its continued employment in the West during the Viking era, and despite a proliferation of images (particularly in the *Utrecht Psalter*) showing the composite bow in use in Europe in the 9th century AD, early-medieval European crossbows were fitted with wooden laths.

Writing between 1180 and 1190, Murḍā al-Tarsūsī, who dedicated a treatise on weapons to Saladin, stated, 'The crossbow ... is fitted with a simple bow without horn or sinew ... It should be of yew of the best kind that grows ... After yew comes wild olive wood, of which there are two varieties, one imported from North Africa, the other from Yemen' (quoted in Paterson 1990: 35). Yew is not surprising and olive wood is interesting, but what is most striking about this statement is that it both acknowledges the existence of composite bows and also declares that they were not used for crossbows.

The engineering of the composite bow for crossbows involved an entirely different stacking arrangement of the materials than was the practice with regular hand-bows. At the time Murḍā al-Tarsūsī was writing, this was an advance that had not yet been developed. Until the very end of the 12th century and possibly not until the 13th century, all European crossbows had wooden laths.

Assessing proportions from art, combined with measurements from the few medieval wooden crossbow laths that have survived, indicates that 4 feet was a common size, though some seem to have been shorter. For any given length of limb there is a limit to the draw-weight attainable for a wooden bow. According to the bowyer Chris Boyton (private correspondence 2017), the maximum draw-weight for a wooden bow, with a span of 4 feet, would probably be around 200lb, and less for shorter bows. At this size a crossbow may be designated a 'great-crossbow' (see below) and so the 200lb estimation is at the extreme upper limit of the scale for a standard crossbow of maximum length. When considering these draw-weights it is important to bear in mind that, unlike a longbow where an archer drawing to the ear will have a draw-length of 30–31 inches, the crossbow has a power-stroke of only around 4–5 inches. Moreover, if we assume that the bow must be spanned several times a minute, repeatedly, for it to be effective on the battlefield, then perhaps a draw-weight of 150lb might be more typical for the average soldier. Spanning devices had yet to appear.

Anna Komnene tells us how the early crossbows were spanned: '[It] has to be stretched by lying almost on one's back; each foot is pressed against the half-circles of the bow and the two hands tug at the bow (string), pulling it with all one's strength towards the body' (Komnene 2009: 282). While a strong man could lean his back into perhaps 250lb with this technique, there remains the mechanical limitation of tillering a short wooden bow above a certain weight without the risk of it breaking.

Surviving wooden-bowed crossbows from the medieval period are extremely rare – those not used for firewood have rotted away – and this can give a misleading impression of their prevalence. They were used extensively throughout the period. Compared to composite bows, wooden bows were simple, quick and economic to manufacture, with readily available materials. They could be produced in considerable numbers and, for both battlefield and garrison troops, they were adequate for the task and required relatively little maintenance in the field. For these reasons, wooden-bowed crossbows remained in general use long after the introduction of

A wooden bow for a crossbow found in 1931 during excavations at Berkhamsted Castle, England, and believed to date to the 13th century. It measures 49 inches. It is a powerful and hefty lath with a stout, deep 'D' section and may be considered to be the lath of a great-crossbow. For obvious reasons few wooden laths survive, but they continued in extensive use throughout the medieval period. (© The Trustees of the British Museum)

composite bows. Guy Wilson (former Master of the Royal Armouries and an eminent crossbow scholar) offers the following summary from primary sources:

> In 1418 the town of Blois had within its armoury crossbows with bows made of Portuguese yew. When the victorious Henry V of England had France at his mercy in 1421 and ordered an inventory to be taken of the arms available in Paris and elsewhere, among the many crossbows found were ten large windlass and ten smaller crossbows, all with bows made of Portuguese yew, as well as five large bows made of something called 'Flemish wood' that may have been Prussian yew. In 1436 22 large wooden crossbows were bought from a Spanish merchant for the Duke of Burgundy; and it was not until 1461 that the town of Tournai replaced its wooden crossbows with steel ones. (Wilson 2007: 322)

In his survey of European crossbows Josef Alm cites a Burgundian inventory from 1362 which lists 189 crossbows with composite bows and 382 crossbows with wooden bows (Alm 1994: 25). He goes on to refer to an order of 7,000 bow-staves of yew to be supplied to the Grand Master of the Teutonic Order for the making of crossbow laths in 1396 (Alm 1994: 27). Furthermore, Burgundian military accounts include crossbows with yew bows for the years 1433, 1437 and 1442 (Alm 1994: 34).

The historian Sir Ralph Payne-Gallwey, in his 1903 magnum opus on the subject, records a translation from a mid-14th-century poem by David-ap-Gwilym, which commences with the following couplet: 'And thou crossbowman true and good / Thou shooter with the faultless wood' (Payne-Gallwey 1981: 6). It offers a suggestion of wooden-bowed crossbows by a contemporary witness. Another, more specific, 14th-century reference dates to 1346, the year of the battle of Crécy: 'Robert Arblaster and Simon Russell were ordered to cut down yew trees in the manor of Easthampstead to make cross-bows' (Cal Pat: 9). It is worth noting the etymological connection between the name Arblaster and the word for a crossbow-maker or crossbowman (arbalist). We also see that, at a time when there had been great demands on stocks of premium timber for Edward III's French adventure, home-grown yew was deemed perfectly suitable for crossbows. Nevertheless, as with longbows, Italian yew was especially desirable. Two

The wooden bow of this crossbow is believed to date to the 13th or 14th century. Both the tiller and the iron fittings are 19th-century substitutions and so no guide to age, or style. Originally, the wooden bow would have been cradled in the fork of a tiller with a strip of leather and bound into place with cords. Also, the metal of the stirrup would not have attached with direct contact to the wooden bow. The bow itself is a magnificent example, however, and, like the Berkhamsted bow, the knots in the wood have been left proud on the back, producing a characteristically knobbly appearance. The bow measures 45.5 inches. (© CSG CIC Glasgow Museums and Libraries Collections)

Genoese merchants were issued a writ in September 1390 for dodging the customs tariffs on '35 tuns of malmsey and 288 staves for crossbows' they had taken to London for sale (CCR Rich II). No less in demand were Iberian supplies, as indicated in the following requisition for 400 yew staves to make crossbows in 1284:

> To Peter de la Mare, constable of Bristol castle. Order to cause to be provided four hundred staves (*baculos*) of Spanish yew to make cross-bows, four hundred nuts (*nuces*), four hundred keys, four hundred 'stirrups' (*stripodia*), a hundred baldricks (*baudreas*), twenty pieces of whalebone (*balena*), a thousand bow-strings (*nervis*), a hundred thousand quarrels for cross-bows for two feet, and a hundred thousand quarrels for cross-bows for one foot, and to cause them to be carried to Kaernarvan, there to be delivered to Master Richard de Abindon, the king's chamberlain there. (CCR Ed I 1284)

Baleen is a cartilage-like material that is made of keratin, a primary constituent of horn. Plates of baleen are situated in the mouths of various species of whale. Bristles attach to these plates to act as a filter when feeding. It is a stiff, strong and springy material. Although known popularly as whalebone, it is not bone. Baleen, from the whale's palate, was used for centuries to back bows in Inuit culture and I suspect that was its intended purpose here. Backing a wooden bow with parchment or similar material by attaching a strip to the back of the bow with a strong adhesive remains a common practice among traditional archers. It relieves the tension stresses on the back of the bow and prevents fibres from lifting, making it less likely to break and rendering it more efficient to shoot. With its inherent elastic properties, baleen would make a superior material for the task and probably also boost performance. It cannot be stated for certain that this is why baleen appears in a list of crossbow-making materials, but it is a possibility. If I am right, then it may be that the baleen was for backing all 400 staves, or it may have been reserved for patching old bows that were showing signs of weakness, thus keeping them going a little longer.

Either way, baleen-backed wooden bows may have been an intermediate technology between wooden bows and true composite bows made with horn. It is possible that baleen-backed bows were able to exceed the typical draw-weight of a simple wooden bow. As with the longbow, small pieces of horn were sometimes used to reinforce the nocks of the more powerful wooden-lathed crossbows.

Taybughā al-Ashrafī al-Baklamishī al-Yūnanī, author of *Kitāb ghunyat at-tullāb fī ma'rifat ramy an-nushshāb* (Essential Archery for Beginners) *c.*1500, noted that for naval operations the most useful type of crossbow is one with a lath made from yew. It is perhaps obvious that wooden bows would be less sensitive to the wet conditions of maritime warfare than a composite bow would be, but he adds interest to the observation by telling us that 'The limb of this weapon should be made of two opposing staves' (quoted in Latham & Paterson 1970: 8).

Wooden bows may also be made by laminating two staves together, either of different woods or the same, and this would seem to be the intended meaning here. Manuscript art sometimes shows differently coloured strata on a bow, which may be an indication of laminate construction. A laminated lath would be more robust, resilient to everyday knocks and bumps, than a true self-bow would be, and would be less prone to breakage. While laminate construction did not, of itself, produce greater power, its dependability might encourage confidence in risking higher draw-weights.

Both wooden bows and composite bows had a limit to how long they remained serviceable in storage, especially if they had seen prior use. Good maintenance was essential. Accounts from the privy wardrobe at the Tower of London in 1353 describe: '4 small crossbows with composite bows, worn out, 59 old and worn out wooden normal crossbows, 4 of which were broken' (Richardson 2016: 150). Here the use of the word 'normal' associated with wooden bows is intriguing. Does it suggest that crossbows with wooden laths represented the mainstream? Despite their commonality, wooden-lathed crossbows were not necessarily considered lower-status weapons because the same entry goes on to inform us that the Tower inventory included '86 new ones with wooden bows, one for the king's personal use' (Richardson 2016: 150).

An ordinance from Germany in 1382 specified a crossbow with 'a bow of yew' to be delivered to the Holy Roman Emperor for a hunting expedition (Alm 1994: 27). In 1553 William Rothwell, keeper of the privy wardrobe at the Tower of London, ordered 200 wooden bow-staves for crossbows at a cost of 26s 8d per hundred – that is 3¼d each. This was exactly the same price he paid for longbow staves. Once fashioned into working bows these same crossbow staves were valued at 6s 8d each. The cost compared favourably with that of composite bows, which the same account records at 20s each (Richardson 2016: 151). Improved technology carried a significant premium.

Composite and horn laths

Although more costly, composite-bow technology offered two distinct advantages over the wooden bow; shorter limbs and more power. With bow lengths ranging typically between 23 and 36 inches, composite bows were much less cumbersome than their wooden antecedents; easier to handle on both battlefield and rampart and far more discreet to manage on the hunting field. The materials and construction design enabled the manufacture of bows with draw-weights that could range from 200lb to 600lb. These greater weights demanded spanning mechanisms with mechanical advantage and these developed in tandem as the strength of bows increased.

The composite bow delivered its power with greater efficiency, so that even a 200lb composite bow was able to shoot a bolt with greater force than could the equivalent weight of wooden bow. A further benefit of the composite bow was that it was more reliable; less prone to shattering than either the wooden bow or the steel bow.

Methods of constructing composite bows for crossbows were wholly different from the way in which composite hand-bows were made (see Loades 2016: 22–26). The breakthrough came in redesigning the composite structure from a simple linear lamination of materials (as was the case with hand-bows) to assembling a complex matrix, which concentrated the power into a shorter, stockier limb and magnified it by having multiple strata of horn. This innovation appears at some point at the end of the 12th or beginning of the 13th centuries, most probably originating in the Middle East; more than 2,500 years after the appearance of hand-bows made with wood, horn and sinew. To all intents and purposes the composite bow for the crossbow was an entirely new invention. Surviving specimens (already in a broken state) in both public and private collections have been sawn to produce clean cross-section views, revealing that a wide variety of construction schemes were employed.

Horn was the key material; it was the source of most of the power and contemporary references referred to these bows as horn-bows. While water-buffalo horn was most prized for the composite hand-bow, composite bows for the European crossbow were more usually built with either cattle or goat horn; materials that were more readily available. Ibex horn was especially favoured.

Bundles of different-sized horn strips were stacked in two layers with each strip fused to its neighbour on both abutting planes. Prior to assembly each length of horn was prepared by using a toothed scraper to cut precision parallel grooves on its surfaces. Bonded together with powerful hide-glue, each piece interlocked with its fellow. The grooves not only offered a larger surface for adhesion but also counteracted the potential for slipping.

FAR LEFT Section of a composite lath from a 15th-century Swiss or German crossbow. The catalogue listing identifies the components as baleen, horn and tendon (sinew) with an outer covering of birch bark. The species of wood at the core has not been identified, but is probably beech. Note the precision-grooved surfaces of both the horn and the wooden billets. These create interlocking toothed parts which give a secure foundation for an adhesive bond and which resist slipping. (Metropolitan Museum of Art, www.metmuseum.org)

LEFT Section of a composite lath from a 15th-century crossbow. Note that this specimen has no wooden core. It has two rows of cattle horn, the strips mixed in both size and pigmentation, and wedge-shaped strips of horn at the outer edges in place of the more usual wooden support. The whole is wrapped in sinew, built up into many layers on the back of the bow. (Image courtesy of Chris Boyton)

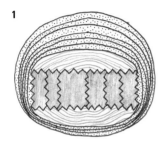
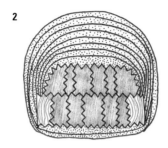
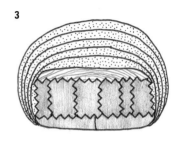

1   2   3

Three variations on the internal construction of a composite lath. One (**1**) has a single layer of horn strips as the core, held in place above and below by wooden billets. The whole is wrapped in sinew. The second example (**2**) has two layers of horn strips, steadied only on the lower row by wooden strips at the sides. It too is covered in multiple layers of sinew. The third example (**3**) is a plan for the cross-section of the Novotny bow (below). It has a central wooden core – beech – identified by wood-grain-style lines; layers of sinew, indicated by the dotted section; and both vertical and horizontal strips of horn, the shaded section. (David Joseph Wright)

Composite-bow lath, built by Lukas Novotny, under construction. Note the reflex of the bow. When strung the tips of the bow, which curve away in this image, will be tensioned inwards towards the viewer. Unfinished and without a covering, the layers of sinew are clearly visible. Horn strips are also visible on the belly – the inner face – of the bow, but what cannot be seen is the internal construction: see above. (Image courtesy of Saluki Bows)

Baleen also featured in some composite bows. Three pieces of baleen were itemized in a comprehensive list of components for the making of 40 composite laths for crossbows in 1345, commissioned by the Tower Armoury (Richardson 2016: 147). It is difficult to determine the extent to which baleen was used in bow manufacture because, in its desiccated form, it has the appearance of dried sinew. Equally hard to discern are its mechanical advantages. Baleen had neither the springiness of horn nor the tensile strength of sinew.

The horn nucleus was encased in layers of sinew, with many extra layers built up on the back of the bow. It was the horn, naturally resistant to compression, which generated the most stored energy when the bow was bent. It was the sinew that held everything together, however. Made from dried animal tendons, soaked in fish-glue, the sinew also contributed an amount of elastic energy to this complex spring.

A third component was wood, but the extent to which it was employed varied from substantial to barely present. There were several different arrangements for the placing of the wood within the matrix, ranging from a robust wooden core to thin strips either side of the horn centre. In some bows, a wooden strip ran either above or below the horn. Compared to the greater forces of horn and sinew, this wooden component probably didn't add anything to the elasticity of the bow. It was there to counteract the potential for the horn cluster to shift or twist. During the manufacturing process it could provide a skeleton on which to build the muscles of horn and the tendons of the sinew, lining everything up while the slow-curing glues set. It offered stability.

Traditional bow-woods such as yew or elm were useful, but the most common timber seems to have been beech. Beech responds extremely well to steaming, which may have a particular advantage for the crossbow lath. To augment the power of composite materials, some bows were made with a prominent reflex; that is to say, the limbs curved away from the shooter in the bow's unstrung state. Steam-bent lengths of wood may have been especially useful in establishing the geometry of a reflex bow. Even so, there is evidence that reflex laths were sometimes made without the stability of a wooden framework. All horns

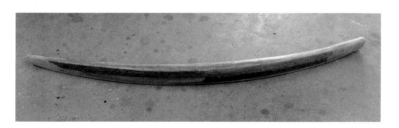

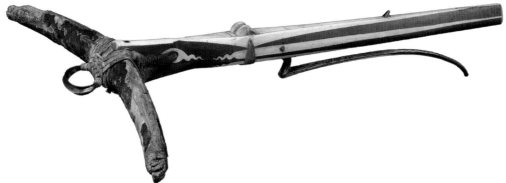

have a natural curve and certainly the long sweeping curve of ibex horn seems especially suited to creating reflex laths; requiring only a modicum of steaming to coax their arcs into symmetrical bends.

Damp conditions had the potential to be deleterious to the glues that were the essential bond between the laminations of a composite structure. In order to protect them from the weather, composite bows were covered and sealed with a varnish.

Steel laths

The earliest mention of a steel crossbow lath appears in 1316, listed in an inventory of goods stolen from Mathilda of Brabant (1268–1329); it was gilded (Breiding 2013: 30). Most probably it was a low-powered prototype with a certain novelty value. Manufacturing a shootable steel lath of low poundage was one thing, but forging one with colossal power was quite another. Experiments with steel bows continued throughout the 14th century, but it was only when they began to exceed the draw-weights possible with composite bows that they began to usurp the military dominance of the older style. Eventually, by the end of the 14th century, it became possible to fabricate steel laths of staggeringly high draw-weights. Slightly in excess of 1,500lb was possible for the larger bows, though most would have been less than this. Even so, at 750lb steel bows offered a significant improvement to the maximum 600lb possible with a composite bow (most were less).

By the end of the first quarter of the 15th century, steel became a more common material for crossbow laths. The durability of steel compared to wood or horn has meant that museum collections have a disproportionate number of surviving specimens. However, the truth is that wooden or composite bows were never entirely replaced by steel laths, at least not until the 17th century, when they became ubiquitous for both hunting and target crossbows.

Significant advances in the production of iron and steel occurred during the 14th century, not only prompting major improvements in the quality of armour but also unleashing the potential of steel to make a powerful spring. A greater understanding of heat treatment, judging the colour of steel in the forge before quenching at exactly the right

This unstrung composite bow, possibly Austrian c.1425–75, shows a large degree of reflex with the limbs at rest. Imagining such stout springs drawn back to the strung position, let alone to full draw, conjures up a sense of this bow's considerable power. Length 37.6 inches; width 29.8 inches; weight 8lb 12oz. In this case the bow has traces of birch bark as its outer layer. Covering materials varied widely and also offered a range of decorative options. They were usually applied in two layers; for instance, a layer of leather topped with an outer skin of parchment. Parchment, vellum, paper, linen, leather and bark were all used as wrappings and all presented a canvas that invited painted embellishment. Parchment, the most common material for the outer layer, was often decorated to simulate snakeskin. Actual snakeskin was also fashionable, viper skin being especially popular. Another commonly used material, particularly in England, was dogfish skin. Whatever the outer layer of the bow, it remained prudent always to carry it with an additional waterproof cover. Crossbows with composite bows continued to find favour on the hunting field long after the development of high-powered steel laths. European nobility are depicted using them throughout both the 15th and 16th centuries, particularly in Northern Europe where the cold weather of the hunting season could cause steel crossbows to shatter – an alarming prospect! (Bashford Dean Memorial Collection, Metropolitan Museum of Art, www.metmuseum.org)

A 15th-century crossbow with a steel lath (A1032) in The Wallace Collection, London. The lath has been blackened, then covered with gilded parchment and painted with red floral motifs. It is held in the tiller by a bridle of hemp cord. By the late 15th century it became increasingly common to mount steel laths in their tillers with metal bow irons. At the fore-end, a gilt-iron hanging ring has been attached with interlaced leather strapping. The entire tiller has been veneered with panels of polished antler, adorned with spectacular figurative relief carvings. These have been enlivened with a girdle of painted coats-of-arms, whose colourful display stands out against the almost white background of the carved panels. The additional weight of steel-lathed crossbows compared unfavourably to the composite bow; one of a number of reasons why high-status hunters continued to prefer the lightweight, portable elegance of the older technology. Moreover, the heavier the lath, the greater the amount of the bow's potential energy required to move it. Therefore steel bows had to be of proportionally higher draw-weights than their composite or wooden counterparts in order to counter this inertia. However, the capacity for steel laths with exceptionally high power to be produced meant that they could outperform this minor limitation by a considerable margin. (© The Wallace Collection, London)

moment, enabled smiths to manipulate molecular structures with enormous sophistication. For crossbow laths, historical blacksmith Hector Cole recommends a uniform orange heat and quenching in brine or vegetable oil before flash-tempering in the fire (private correspondence 2017).

Also during the 14th century it became possible to produce cleaner steels with higher carbon contents. Clean steels contain a minimum of slag inclusions; that is, the porridge of silica and elemental impurities that are part of the mix when blooms of iron are smelted from the ore in the first stages of steel production. If left present, these impurities create weak spots where the steel would fracture under stress. The art of the smith in forging a lath for a crossbow was to create a piece of metal that was tempered to possess both strength and elasticity and also to be as homogenous as possible. Furthermore, shaping the lath to have a profile that tapered towards the tips, with symmetrical precision on both limbs, ensured an even distribution of strain throughout the bow when in use.

Although it took considerable skill to forge a steel lath, it was a far quicker process than manufacturing a composite prod, which required not only rare skills but also months of drying times for the all-important glues at various stages of construction. Steel laths could be hammered out in a matter of a few hours and were bow ready as soon as they had cooled from the final temper. They were made from a single, readily available, recyclable material. When produced on a large scale, steel laths were far less costly than composite bows.

Flanders was a traditional centre for crossbow manufacture throughout the Middle Ages and beyond. Among the many entries for 'crossbow thread' (which was presumably hemp cord for crossbow strings and bridles) shown on bills of lading from 16th-century Antwerp, is a listing for '100 lbs of crossbow laths' (LPB). Trading by weight only makes sense with regard to steel laths. Cost presumably related to the amount of metal being sold rather than the quantity of laths – heavier draw-weight bows would have required thicker laths. One assumes that laths were of fairly uniform quality, unless they were blanks and yet to be tempered.

Gilles Le Bouvier, a French chronicler, did not trust steel bows in the cold and, in 1455, extolled the virtues of the composite bow for snowier climes: 'These people [Bavarians] are good crossbowmen on horseback and on foot, and shoot with crossbows of horn and sinew, which are good and strong and do not break when they are frozen, for the colder it is the stronger they are' (quoted in Payne-Gallwey 1981: 64). Steel-lathed crossbows never replaced either wooden or composite laths entirely, but they did become the most universal type during the final half-century of that weapon's useful military service – a period when they competed with the fire and fury of gunpowder weapons.

Deterring rust

Rust was to be greatly feared with a steel lath; any weakness and the bow could break under strain. Given the high draw-weights of steel bows such a breakage would have been a violent event. Consequently, various measures were employed to deter rust. One simple measure was to paint the lath, but more advanced techniques involved blackening the steel by heat treatment. As with composite bows, steel laths were also covered with leather or other material; though this ran the risk of rust developing undetected. All crossbows could be given extra protection for travelling by slipping them into a waterproof case made from waxed leather or canvas. This covered either the entire crossbow or, often, just the strung lath. In 1239 the Constable of Chester paid 5s for canvas to cover the king's crossbows (Blackmore 1971: 181).

A curiosity on surviving steel laths is that they are sometimes adorned with small silk pom-poms. These cluster around the bridle and sometimes also appear on each extremity of the bow-limbs as well as on the trigger lever. Surviving examples (see page 77) can be seen on many hunting crossbows in museums. The hunting context is perhaps a clue. It may be that these pom-poms were a form of camouflage, breaking up the lines of the crossbow's silhouette. It is also a possibility that they acted in the manner of buckskin fringing, wicking and guttering rain away so that it didn't pool and precipitate rust, especially where it could not be seen under the bridle.

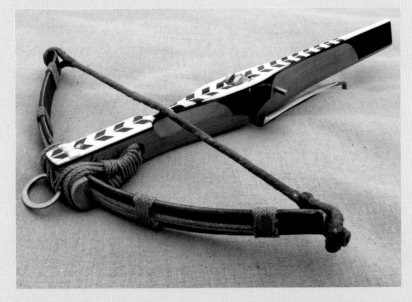

Replica 15th-century crossbow by Leo Todeschini. Note that the steel lath has been fitted with safety cords. Steel bows were often covered with leather or other material, not only to protect against rust but also to minimize the risk of flying steel splinters if the bow shattered. Steel bows were prone to fracture with or without rust. An alternative method of containing these airborne shards was to bind the lath with safety cords. A braided cord was glued to the front of the bow and this was held securely in place with a series of whip bindings at intervals of several inches. (Photograph: Tod's Stuff)

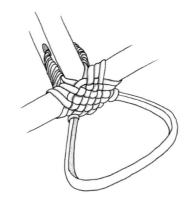

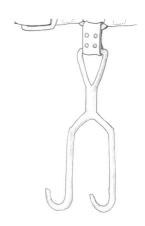

SPANNING AIDS

The stirrup

As noted previously, early crossbows were spanned by sitting and placing both feet on the bow. A solution to this sedentary inconvenience was the introduction of the stirrup at some point in the 12th century, which allowed the shooter to remain standing while performing the same procedure. In the West, the stirrup was fashioned from iron, but both Mamluk crossbows (see page 50) and some Chinese crossbows were fitted with stirrups made from cord.

German sources in the 14th century distinguish between the stirrup crossbow (*Steigreifarmbrust*) and the 'back' crossbow (*Ruckarmbrust*): 'In 1307 and 1308, ten back crossbows (*balistas dorsales*) and ten foot-loop crossbows were purchased for the city of Hamburg' (Alm 1994: 26). One speculative explanation for the difference is that, when hand-spanning, the stirrup/foot-loop crossbow was bent by using one's arms to pull back the string and that it was only when equipped with a belt-and-claw that the arbalist really put his back into it. Another possibility is that the back-crossbow was spanned by sitting and placing both feet on the bow. It seems certain that this practice continued beyond the introduction of the stirrup as the fellow in the margins of the *Luttrell Psalter* (page 20) confirms.

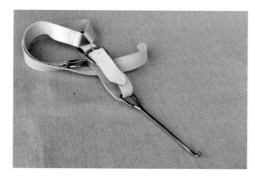

Neither the goat's foot lever nor the cranequin required the assistance of a stirrup, and bows intended for use with these devices were equipped with a hanging-ring instead of a stirrup. Crossbows were stored, whether in castle guardrooms or great state arsenals, by hanging them by either the stirrup or the hanging-ring.

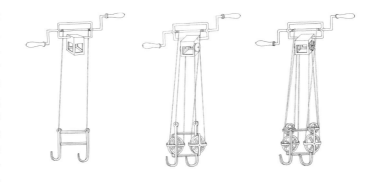

At left is a simple windlass that delivers a power advantage of approximately 10:1. The windlass in the centre is augmented by a single pulley block, delivering a power advantage of roughly 30:1. The windlass on the right has an additional pulley block, which generates a massive power advantage of around 45:1. (David Joseph Wright)

The belt-and-claw system

Consisting of an iron hook attached to an adjustable strip of leather that hung vertically from a waist-belt, the belt-and-claw system is first mentioned in the work of Murḍā al-Tarsūsī c.1180. In English medieval accounts it was referred to as a baldric. The baldric was the simplest of spanning aids and its use continued for military crossbows until the very end of the 15th century, despite the introduction of other, more powerful contraptions. Not only was the belt-and-claw easy and relatively quick to operate, it was significantly less expensive to produce.

There was a limitation to the draw-weight the belt-and-claw could assist. I suspect that most bows used with this system were around 150lb draw-weight, though 200lb might have been possible for strong men. An important factor would be how long the crossbowmen were expected to maintain a constant work rate. For most munition-grade crossbows, the belt-and-claw remained the standard system throughout the medieval period.

The windlass

The windlass, or winch, was the heavy-lifting workhorse of medieval artillery and it manifested in a number of forms. With the advent of composite laths, higher draw-weights became possible. It was the windlass that enabled the development of these more powerful weapons and for that to continue into the next generation of high-powered steel laths.

First appearing at some point in the 13th century, the early windlass was a simple capstan without pulleys. A box-like metal cap fitted to the butt of the tiller. Attached to this cap was a frame, housing the capstan and the winding handles. Cords extended to the hooking tackle. In operation the arbalist steadied the bow on the ground by means of the stirrup and wound the handles. Once the bow was spanned he had to reverse the winding by a few turns to create enough slack to disengage the hooks.

Once it became possible to make bows of extreme power, after the development of steel bows, the primary form of the windlass was boosted with additional pulleys. The more pulleys, the greater the length of cord and the greater the potential for entanglements when this winding gear was laid on the ground between loading procedures. The windlass crossbowman had to be both methodical and adept at handling his tackle. There was a knack to it and modern tests have shown that a reasonably practised person can manage to load and shoot a bolt in a fraction above 30 seconds. Rather than saying two bolts a minute, it might be safer to suggest eight bolts in five minutes for the most powerful crossbows.

In order to situate the winding gear at an ergonomic height for the arbalist, windlass crossbows had longer tillers. This, together with the windlass itself, made them bulky and awkward, far more suited to the static conditions of a siege than to the battlefield. Although superseded by the more sophisticated and far more powerful cranequin, the windlass crossbow continued to see service. A 1523 inventory of the goods of Lord Mounteagle included two windlasses for crossbows (LPFD Hen VIII 3).

The cord-and-pulley system

A simpler, and much quicker, device, that also offered the mechanical advantage of a pulley, was the cord-and-pulley system, which came into use in the early 15th century, possibly a decade or so earlier. Although it looks to be the probable antecedent of the windlass, current evidence suggests that it appeared later.

By the measure of other devices such as the windlass or the cranequin, the cord-and-pulley system did not offer a huge power advantage. Even so, at a ratio of 2:1 it did enable a man to use a 300lb bow with relative ease and frequency. Slower than the belt-and-claw but quicker than other mechanical systems, it was a useful, inexpensive and lightweight apparatus suitable for medium-weight bows. According to Alm, the 'Sampson belt', as he calls it, was particularly popular in Sweden during the 15th century (Alm 1994: 41).

Crossbows spanned in this manner are depicted in *The Martyrdom of Saint Sebastian* by Antonio del Pollaiuolo, *c*.1432–98 (National Gallery, London) and it is clear that their bows are not fitted with stirrups. With one hand on the end of the tiller, they steady their weapons by stepping over the bow with one foot, cradling the lath between the heel of the forward leg and the shin of the rear leg. In this instance they are using a single cord with a single pulley and hook.

The cord-and-pulley. These drawings show a twin-hooked pulley block. Some examples had just a single pulley with a single hook. One end of the cord was attached to a waist-belt and the other had a ring, which slipped onto a hook fixed to the underside of the crossbow's tiller. Running along the cord was the pulley fitted with the hook(s). By bending his knees, the arbalist was able to lower himself a little to engage the string with the pulley-hook(s). Straightening his legs by standing up spanned the bow, with the pulley delivering a 2:1 power advantage. (David Joseph Wright)

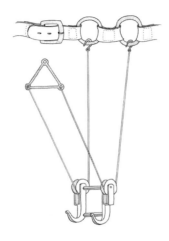
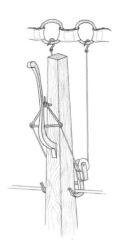

Gaffle or goat's foot lever, late 15th or early 16th century. The surfaces of each lever are decorated with simple punched designs. There is also decorative file work on the bridge and the grapple. Note the hook attachment for carrying it on a belt. When the device is folded the suspension hook swivels 90 degrees both to secure the ends of the twin levers and to orientate the carrying hook for its purpose. Length extended 19.6 inches; width 2.8 inches; weight 25oz. The claw hooked over the string and the terminals of the curved fork braced against stout pins that protruded either side of the crossbow tiller. When the hinged lever arm was pulled towards the butt of the stock, the fork acted against the pins, applying the leverage required to draw back the string. The gaffle delivered a mechanical advantage of around 5:1. (Metropolitan Museum of Art, www.metmuseum.org)

The gaffle

Bending levers, known originally as gaffles, took various forms, both fixed and hinged. The alternative nomenclature – goat's foot lever – derived its name from the curve of the lever arms that resembled the hind legs of a goat. With a mechanical advantage of 5:1, these benders were powerful tools that were also quick to use. Modern experiments conducted by Leo Todeschini have demonstrated that it is possible to shoot five bolts a minute using this device on a crossbow of 300lb draw-weight.

Gaffles do not seem to be represented in art before the middle of the 14th century but are well known thereafter, remaining in use throughout the 15th century, especially for hunting bows and for mounted crossbowmen. Despite their efficiency, gaffles were not employed extensively on the battlefield during the 14th century; the less-expensive belt-and-claw system continued to dominate. Gaffles did, however, gain favour in defending fortifications, offering greater speed than the windlass and greater mechanical assistance than the belt-and-claw.

A variation, which enabled the arbalist to exert greater force, featured a curved 'T' at the terminus of the lever. This was braced against the crossbowman's thigh, allowing him to grasp the tiller of his bow with both hands and pull using his back and arms. Examples are rare, though there is one in the Berne Historical Museum. Instances of its use can be seen in Italian art, for which reason it is sometimes known as the Italian type.

The cranequin

According to W.F. Paterson, the earliest record of a cranequin is in 1373 (Paterson 1990: 51) and its use reaches a peak during the 15th and 16th centuries. Utilizing gear wheels cut with engineering precision, the cranequin was the most powerful of all crossbow-spanning devices. It was also the most sophisticated and expensive. It had other names, the

A fine example of a high-status cranequin (A1054). Both the gear casing and the ratchet bar have been etched and gilded. Note the hook for carrying the device on a belt. Cranequins enjoyed particular prestige, not only because they gave unrivalled mechanical advantage but also because they represented state-of-the-art precision engineering. The cranequin consisted of a geared winding block that travelled along a toothed ratchet bar. A claw to engage the string was located at one end of the ratchet bar and a thick cord bridle was attached to the winding block. This bridle slipped over the end of the tiller to be arrested by protruding pins on either side; thus as the mechanism was wound it moved the ratchet bar to retract the string. (© The Wallace Collection, London)

rack or the cric, and there were regional variations. The 'German winder' had teeth cut into the side of the ratchet bar with the gearbox mounted on top, so that the handle turned parallel to the lath of the crossbow; whereas the 'French winder' or 'Spanish winder' was mounted in such a way that the handle turned at right angles to the lath, parallel to the tiller.

When a cranequin in the collections of the Metropolitan Museum of Art, New York was tested on a crossbow of 1,090lb, it required only 7.5lb force applied to the handle in order to draw the bow – a mechanical advantage of 145:1 (Paterson 1990: 52). The complex gearing on individual cranequins varied considerably, but it seems probable that 145:1 is at the upper end of what was achievable.

Despite its clear advantages, the cranequin was relatively slow to use and somewhat heavy to carry around. It was even rather noisy, though this did not reduce its popularity among high-status hunters. Of course, if you were of sufficiently high status, you had someone else to do the winding for you.

Spanning, c.1400 (opposite)

By 1400 a range of mechanical spanning devices was available, allowing bows of greater power to be developed. The windlass (top left) first appeared as early as the 13th century. The number of pulleys varied. This one, with a single set of wheels, generated a power advantage of 30:1. Here it is being used to span a composite lath of around 600lb draw-weight. The cord-and-pulley (top right) was a much later development than the windlass, only appearing at the beginning of the 15th century. It offered a power advantage of 2:1. Here it is being used to span a composite lath of around 200lb draw-weight. The gaffle, or goat's foot lever (below left), was known from the mid-14th century, but did not occur frequently until the 15th century. It gave a power advantage of 5:1. Here it is being used to span a composite-lath of 300lb draw-weight. The cranequin (centre right), the most powerful of all spanning mechanisms, was developed during the last quarter of the 14th century. Some versions had the potential for a 145:1 power advantage. Here it is being used to span the new technology of the steel lath, with a draw-weight of 800lb.

Not only did the cranequin carry the prestige of great expense and the cachet of cutting-edge technology, its large metal surfaces lent themselves to elaborate artistic embellishment. Many cranequins were exquisite works of art, featuring pierced, punched, chiselled, filed, etched and gilded decoration. More utilitarian examples existed for use by regular troops. Nevertheless, it is generally true to say that the cranequin came into existence at a time when the crossbow's military usefulness was already in decline. Cranequins were to be seen more often in the hunting field or at the shooting ground than on the battlefield.

The screw

Though depictions are rare in medieval art, the screw or 'vice' is mentioned frequently in 14th-century documents. Below is a selection of entries extracted from the records of the privy wardrobe at the Tower of London:

> 4 one-foot composite crossbows and one of wood with screw mechanism (1330)
> 2 old screw winders for the crossbows (1330)
> 32 crossbows in another batch, two of them screw crossbows (1340)
> 14 composite bows with screws (1353)
> 12 screw crossbows (1553)
> 3 screw winders for crossbows (1360)
> seven screw crossbows and of these three large (1360)
> 7 screw crossbows and 3 additional screws for crossbows (1364)
> 1 great composite screw crossbow with a length of 6 feet (1375)
> (Richardson 2016: 144–153)

From these listings it appears that the screw mechanism was used as a device for crossbows of a standard size as well as for great-crossbows. From its frequent appearance in inventories, it would seem that the screw was in greater use than is portrayed in art.

The amount of mechanical advantage offered by the screw mechanism depended on the pitch of the thread. This would have varied and, without surviving examples, is difficult to determine. Presumably it was of adequate assistance, albeit fairly slow. Where inventories list 'screw winders' it is hard to know if this is an alternative descriptor for the entire screw mechanism or whether they are referring to the handwheels as separate elements. Certainly the length of the arms on these handwheels would be a factor in creating mechanical advantage, particularly on versions for the great-crossbow, where the longer arms, usually four, acted as significant levers.

Known as the vice in medieval documents, the screw could be either a detachable mechanism (as illustrated here) or incorporated into the bow itself. A housing fitted over the end of the tiller. Through this passed a threaded rod, which had a claw at one end to catch over the bowstring and a handwheel at the other end. As the handwheel was turned, engaging the thread of the screw within the housing, the rod retracted, drawing back the string. Once the string was located behind the nut, the handwheel was spun in the opposite direction, allowing the claw and rod to be removed. (David Joseph Wright)

One-foot and two-foot crossbows

There are frequent mentions in contemporary sources of 'one-foot crossbows' (*arbalistae ad unum pedem*) and 'two-foot crossbows' (*arbalistae ad duos pedes*). According to W.F. Paterson (Paterson 1990: 38), who follows the thinking of earlier authors such as Payne-Gallwey, this distinction related to the width of the stirrup, with the two-foot versions able to accommodate two feet instead of one. A problem with this analysis is that no images in contemporary art show two feet together in a stirrup and common sense dictates that such a stance would cause a standing crossbowman to lose his balance during spanning, occasioning much mirth among his enemies.

Primary sources often cite two-foot crossbows with specific reference to crossbows spanned with a windlass. An order for crossbows and other armaments to be procured for the defence of Porchester Castle in 1326 reads: '100 crossbows with windlass (*de turno*) for two feet, 200 cross-bows for one foot, with baldrics (*baldredis*)' (CCR Ed II). Here, and in many other instances, there is a clear distinction between the two-foot crossbows, requiring the power of a windlass, and the one-foot crossbows, which were for use with baldrics; that is to say the belt-and-claw system. The association of a windlass with a two-foot crossbow certainly confounds any idea that the term related to the older practice of lying on one's back to span the bow with both feet on the lath. Nevertheless, we have to be cautious when interpreting references to 'windlass' crossbows, unless there is other context. It may be that the author intended a 'great-crossbow' (a crossbow of 'two-feet') or it may be that the reference was to a normal-sized 'one-foot' crossbow, powerful enough to require a windlass. The designations 'great-crossbow' and 'two-foot crossbow' refer only to size. It remained possible to have a 'one-foot crossbow' spanned by the type of portable windlass tackle described previously. The term 'windlass', in the context of a great-crossbow, referred to a similar winding mechanism incorporated into a spanning bench.

Wooden, horn and steel laths are all mentioned in the records for bows of either type, so materials were not a determining factor for the 'foot' taxonomy. There was, however, a price distinction. In 1305, in England, the cost of a one-foot crossbow was 3s 6d compared to 5s for a two-foot crossbow and 8s for a three-foot crossbow (Blackmore 1971: 183, 362n). To date this is the only known reference to a three-foot crossbow and it suggests a classification according to size, with larger, more powerful crossbows being, as we would expect, more expensive. Currently, the most widely believed explanation proposes that the terms indicate a distinction between a crossbow of standard size that shoots a bolt of 'one-foot' in length and a 'great-crossbow' that shoots a 'two-foot' bolt (Liebel 1998: 24). This theory includes the persuasive argument that there was a benefit in standardizing the size of ammunition for crossbows; notwithstanding that there was some size differentiation, even between crossbows of a similar type. The head of a crossbow bolt or quarrel protrudes in front of the crossbow itself. This not only allows the shaft to sit flat, but also avoids any damage that an iron head might cause to the surface of the bow. Crossbow ammunition is therefore not a critical fit. It would also be a simple matter for the individual crossbowman to make a small adjustment of a half-inch or so for optimal balance. Having two basic categories of quarrel size makes complete sense for mass-procurement, with more outsize versions being by bespoke order. Relatively few records specify requisitions for quarrels according to type (either according to the 'foot' classification or for windlass crossbows); the vast majority of orders are non-specific with regard to size (Wilson 2007: 317). The presumption is that, unless otherwise stated, the order would be for one-foot crossbows. Certainly, one-foot crossbows were invariably ordered in greater numbers than were two-foot crossbows. For instance, an order to the sheriffs of London in 1288 enjoined them to send 'forty good cross-bows for one foot and four cross-bows for two feet' (CCR Ed I 1288) to the constable of Bristol Castle. Four decades later, in 1328, the sheriffs of London were ordered to send '100 foot-crossbows, and 20 crossbows with windlasses' (CCR Ed III) to Portsmouth. Expense was doubtless part of the calculation, but one-foot crossbows could be spanned and shot much more speedily and used in a more versatile set of circumstances. The great-crossbow was a specialist weapon.

OTHER TYPES OF CROSSBOW

The great-crossbow

Great-crossbows were outsize versions of the standard crossbow. Jean Liebel, who to date has written the only work dedicated to the subject, tracks their genesis to the early 11th century (Liebel 1998: 25). Great-crossbows continued in universal use until at least the mid-15th century, especially for the defence of castles, towns and cities. Though used primarily as rampart bows, great-crossbows were also employed by besieging armies for attack.

Liebel catalogued a number of known specimens, giving measurements for the length of their laths as: 5 feet 3 inches, 5 feet 9 inches, 6 feet 1 inch, 6 feet 2 inches and 6 feet 6 inches (Liebel 1998: 25). The varying sizes within this small sample are consistent with the range of sizes for great-crossbows that appear in art. While substantially larger than standard crossbows, their modest measurements contrast starkly with those of Leonardo da Vinci's drawings for the design of 'great-crossbows', which had lath measurements of 27 feet 6 inches and 82 feet respectively (Liebel 1998: 25). These were clearly outside the normal range and it is unlikely that such massive bows were ever made.

Some great-crossbows had steel laths, such as the twelve 'great-crossbows of steel' stationed at Orléans in 1419 and 1427 (Liebel 1998: 35). The majority of great-crossbows had either wooden or horn laths, however. At this large scale, the difference in weight between steel and either wood or horn was significant. The choice between wood and horn was determined largely by cost. Composite laths were superior, but more expensive. In 1313, in Artois, in the same transaction for two crossbows of equal size, the horn-bowed crossbow was priced at 2 livres, whereas one with a wooden lath cost only 1 livre (Liebel 1998: 24).

Listed in 14th-century accounts of the Tower Armoury are numerous mentions of *hancepes* in connection with spanning larger crossbows

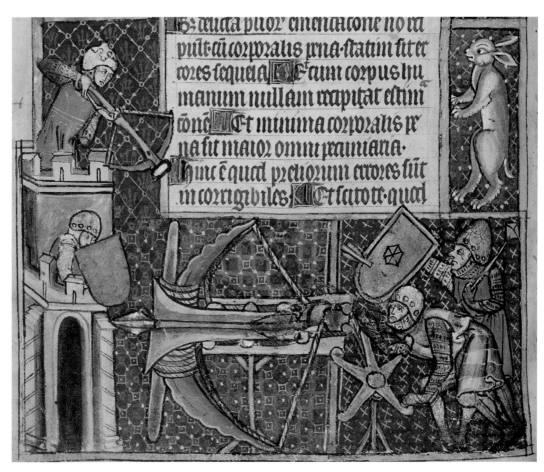

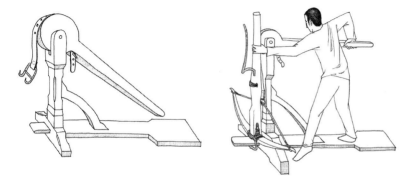

(Richardson 2016: 145). It is a term that does not occur elsewhere but it is strikingly similar to the word *haussepied*, which appears regularly in French records and has been identified as a spanning stand (Liebel 1998: 43). Documents in Latin use either *ausepearum* or *auceprem* in the same context. In 1358, in a dramatic departure from the policies of earlier pontiffs, Pope Innocent VI (r. 1352–62) ordered '30 auceprems' for spanning the great-crossbows that defended his castle at Avignon (Liebel 1998: 48). Spanning stands (*hancepes*) were notably less expensive than the more complex, screw-threaded vice mechanism. Tower records from 1353 record the cost of a *hancepes* at 5s compared to 13s 4d for a vice for a great-crossbow (Richardson 2016: 151).

An inventory from 1445, recording armaments for the defence of Dijon, lists various great-crossbows (*grosses arbalestes*) with bows of yew. One was described as '"*une vielle arbaleste gemelle*" – an old twin crossbow' (Alm 1994: 37). Alm suggests that it was designed to shoot two bolts simultaneously, whereas Liebel considers these 'twin-crossbows' were fitted with two laths (Liebel 1998: 55). Twin-crossbows are also referenced at Metz in 1402 (Liebel 1998: 36). By the 15th century, gunpowder artillery had begun to usurp the long-range role of the great-crossbow, though it is of note that a 1505 inventory of the Hôtel de Ville in Paris counted '48 great steel crossbows' and '5 great crossbows of yew' among its armaments (Liebel 1998: 56).

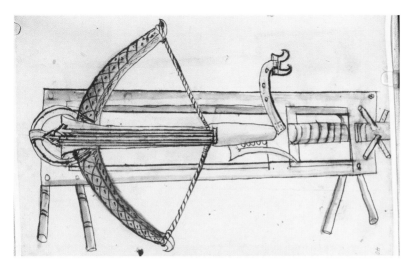

Great-crossbow (for three bolts), mounted on a bench and tensioned by means of a vice. In 1353 Robin of York and other engineers of London supplied 11 screw-threaded mechanisms at 13s 4d each, specifically for great-crossbows (Richardson 2016: 151). The vice or screw was a common apparatus for great-crossbows and, depending on the pitch of the thread, it allowed great-crossbows of considerable power to be spanned by one man; albeit slowly. (Bayerische Staatsbibliothek München, Clm 197,I, fol. 40r)

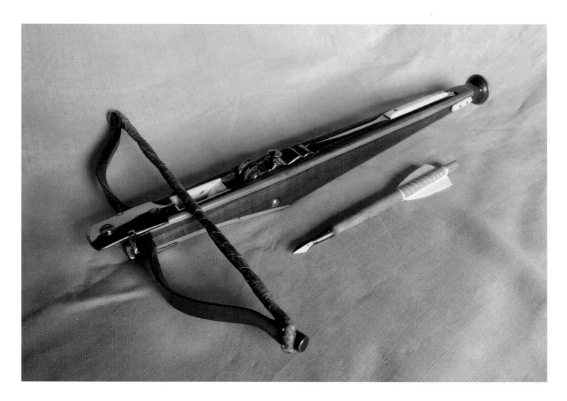

The latchet

During the 16th century, small crossbows of moderate power – seldom more than 200lb – were developed for specific use by horsemen. Known as latchets, they had an inbuilt spanning lever making them simple and fast to span; an action that could be accomplished while holding the reins and the lightweight tiller with one hand and operating the spanning lever with the other. A thumb-trigger was mounted on top of the tiller, making it possible to shoot one-handed.

In the borderlands between Scotland and England, this weapon was known as the 'latch', and was among the arsenal carried by the Border Reivers. During the 16th century these hard-riding marauders were considered among the finest light cavalry in Europe, in addition to their more nefarious reputation as robbers and rustlers. A latch was not only a useful weapon of stealth on a cattle raid, it was also a dependable back-up to the – not-always-

Two views of a replica 16th-century latchet built by Leo Todeschini. The inbuilt spanning lever lifts to enable the grapple to catch the string and the bow is fully prepared by pulling the lever back to locate within the tiller. The thumb-trigger on top is sprung and so automatically resets after shooting. Its power is limited not so much by what was possible for a small steel lath, but rather by the short length of string travel. Even so, it could be effective when shot at close range by a horseman. The lath on this example is 13.5 inches wide. (Photographs: Tod's Stuff)

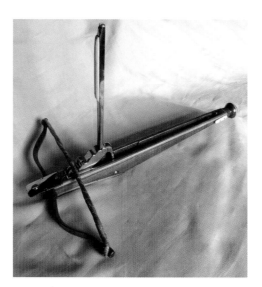

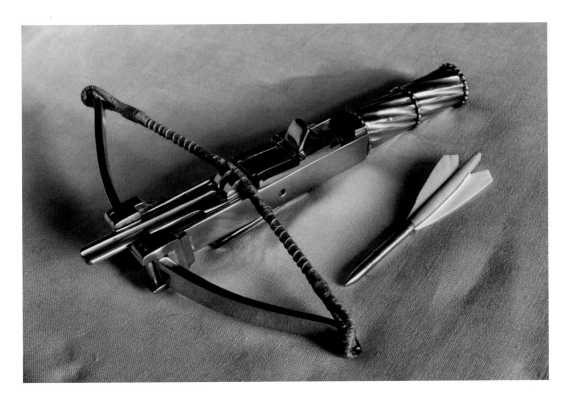

reliable – wheel-lock pistols that the Reivers carried. Latchets also served as easy-to-use personal defence weapons, for folk of modest means wishing to protect their homes.

The *balestrino*

Balestrino means 'small crossbow' in Italian and is the only historical name we have for these tiny bows that first appeared in Spain and Italy during the 16th century. They are also popularly known as the 'assassin's crossbow' but this is a modern term. *Ballestrini* were more powerful than their size would suggest. All were fabricated entirely in steel and spanned by an integral screw mechanism that operated a sliding trigger block. In the same way that a screw-jack for a car can lift enormous weight for little effort, these screw-operated contraptions were able to function with a steel lath in excess of 300lb; albeit it had a very short power-stroke – less than a couple of inches. Surviving examples are rare but to give an idea of scale there is a 16th-century original in the Metropolitan Museum of Art, New York that measures just 11.5 inches in length with a lath of 8.6 inches. Compact and easily concealed, quiet and packing enough punch to pierce an unarmoured man at close range, these little weapons were clearly suitable for the dark work of the assassin, especially if used with poisoned bolts. To date, no accounts of their use in this context have come to light, however, and modern scholars consider it more likely that they were novelty items for the wealthy to play with – toys. Who can doubt the fun of them?

Made by Leo Todeschini, this small crossbow is based on an amalgam of designs from several surviving examples. This powerful little bow (320lb) is spanned with an integral screw mechanism, which functions in conjunction with a sliding block. In this case the turning handle is a cylinder but another common style was for the winder to be in the shape of a winged clock-key. A thumb-trigger is set on top. Length 10.8 inches, lath 8.8 inches. The form of the bolt is speculative, but for a short-range weapon like this, it makes sense to use a heavier bolt. The additional weight of the steel fore-shaft would make an infinitesimal difference to the speed of the bolt at close range, but the extra mass would impart greater impact to the target. (Photograph: Tod's Stuff)

USE
Steady, steady, steady: shoot

THE CROSSBOW IN CHINA

Crossbows and chariots

When men first strained their backs pulling crossbow strings on the battlefield, it was chiefly in order to use their crossbows as anti-chariot weapons. The development of precision bronze casting in China had enabled the mass-production of crossbow locks, which in turn had led to the recruitment and equipping of mass armies on a scale never seen before. China's first Emperor, Qin Shi Huang (259–210 BC), deployed rough regiments of crossbowmen in colossal numbers against the chariot squadrons of his enemy's nobility.

Shooting a regular bow took years of training. It was an art. With the invention of a sophisticated lock mechanism, however, you could fit a bow to a stock – you could make a crossbow – and a man could be taught to shoot a crossbow in a matter of minutes. Speedy training together with a ready supply of crossbows led to the recruitment of mass armies. Tens of thousands of peasants were pressed into military service. Against such impenetrable masses and such an intense barrage of missiles, the chariot was increasingly ineffective. Crossbows, together with the more agile horse-archer, were the chariot's nemesis and by c.250 BC the chariot bells had fallen silent on China's battlefields. Before then, however, during the latter part of the Qin Dynasty, the crossbow had begun also to replace the hand-bow as the weapon of the chariot-archer.

Crossbows took longer to load than hand-bows and could not achieve the same rate of shooting. Rapid shooting techniques with the hand-bow, combined with the hit-and-run dash of a galloping chariot, gave the early chariot-archer considerable battlefield versatility. By contrast, shooting crossbows on the move would have been an inefficient use of the chariot.

The rail of a Qin Dynasty chariot is around knee-height. When standing with flexed knees as is necessary to balance on a moving chariot, it is perfectly possible to stand and shoot, either on the move or with the chariot at a standstill. However, the low rail invites the archer to kneel and to steady himself with one knee against the top rail and the foot of his other leg against the uprights. In this position he has a clear shot over the heads of the horses and yet minimizes himself as a target. (Photograph by Han Zhang)

It could be done, but the team would exert more effort and cover too great a distance between individual shots. Although we do not have precise documentary evidence, it seems more likely that the crossbow was used from static chariots. A chariot still offered the advantage of mobility to deploy quickly on the battlefield, but I suspect that chariots were laagered into standing formations once in position. In support of this idea the archaeological record shows an increase in the length of associated *ji* (halberds) coinciding with the use of the crossbow by chariot warriors.

Chinese chariot crews were comprised of three men: a driver, an archer and a *rongyou*. The latter was really a mounted infantryman, charged with the defence of the chariot in hand-to-hand combat. He was armed with a *ji*. In the earlier period this was no more than 8 feet in length and could be wielded from the chariot platform. However, at the time when the crossbow supplanted the hand-bow on chariots, archaeological finds show a vastly increased length in the *ji* – ranging to as much as 14 feet. It

The biggest challenge of using a crossbow on a Chinese chariot is that of spanning. Qin Dynasty crossbows were comparatively large and had to be spanned by bracing the lath against the feet. By contrast the space on a chariot platform, which accommodated three people (driver, crossbowman, *rongyou*), was extremely compact. One possibility, as demonstrated here by the author, was for the *rongyou* to act as a loader and to sit with his feet hanging from the back. In this way he could span the bow and pass it to the crossbowman. It is a system that would have worked whether deployed in a static position or on the move. (Photograph by Han Zhang)

is awkward and impractical to use a polearm of this size from the platform. Consequently, I believe it was intended that the *rongyou* dismounted to lead the defence of his chariot in a fixed position. In addition to the *rongyou*, 25 running infantry accompanied each chariot. When in static formation, chariots could be vulnerable to an onrush of enemy cavalry. Arraying support infantry with a bristling porcupine of long *ji* was a solution to such a threat and allowed Chinese chariots to be effective shooting platforms for the crossbow.

In the *Romance of Wu an Yue*, written in the 1st century AD, Chen Yin describes the fundamentals of shooting the crossbow:

> The basic form of all shooting is: the body is as erect as if it were held in a wooden frame; the head relaxed like a pebble rolling in the stream; the left foot aligned with the target; the right foot at right angles to the target; the left hand as if glued to the grip; right arm as if cradling a baby; you raise the crossbow towards the enemy; draw your concentration together as you inhale and then shoot in coordination with your breathing so that the whole series of actions is in harmony. Your inner mind is settled and all conscious thoughts must be driven out. There must be absolute separation of those parts which move from those which don't: the right hand pulls the trigger and the left hand never reacts, as if one body were controlled by totally different impulses set at opposing extremes. (Quoted in Selby 2000: 160)

On the one hand this description evokes the highest principles of aristocratic martial arts, such as empty-mindedness; yet on the other hand the context makes it clear that this is prosaic instruction for the masses. Qin's Terracotta Army contains a large number of crossbowmen, all of whom assume a posture exactly as described by Chen Yin.

Volley-shooting

A singular advantage of the crossbow is that once spanned it can be held far longer before shooting than is possible with a powerful hand-bow – although there is some trade-off between holding it spanned for too long and the lath beginning to lose power, especially with wooden bows. Not only did this ability confer clear advantages upon both the hunter and the sniper, it also gave rise to the possibility of volley-shooting. An early example of this was recorded in Sima Qian's account of the battle of Maling (342 BC). Sun Bin placed 10,000 crossbowmen in concealed positions either side of a defile. Their instructions were to 'shoot together if you see a fire lit' (quoted in Selby 2000: 171). The enemy, under Pang Juan, arrived at the pass at twilight. Sun Bin had stripped a tree of its bark, laid it on the road and written 'Pang Juan will perish under this tree' on the white wood. Straining to read the message, Pang Juan had torches lit. Instantly Sun Bin's crossbowmen unleashed a devastating volley, resulting in victory.

In the *Tai bai yin jing*, a Tang Dynasty (618–907) military manual from AD 759, there is a drawing illustrating a drill for volley-shooting by rotating ranks of crossbowmen. The front-line rank of 'shooting crossbowmen' cycles with a second rank of 'loading crossbowmen'. Drummers are shown, commanding the actions to a regimented beat. Writing half a century later, in the *Tong dian* (AD 802), the scholar Du You explained that, 'They take turns, revolving and returning, so that once they've loaded they exit [to the outer ranks] and once they've shot they enter [to within the formation]. In this way the sound of the crossbow will not cease and the enemy will not harm us' (quoted in Andrade 2016: 150).

By the 11th century, just as the military crossbow was becoming established in Europe, Chinese tacticians had introduced a third rank of 'advancing' crossbows to the rotation in between the loaders and the shooters. This three-rank system endured to at least the end of the Ming Dynasty. In 1621 Cheng Chongdou, a student of the Shaolin Temple, wrote that

> The ancients used ten thousand crossbows shooting in concert to win victories over enemies … The first hundred men, which is to say the 'shooting crossbows' shoot. After they are done they retire to the rear, at which the second hundred men, the 'advancing crossbows', move to the fore and themselves become 'shooting crossbows' … and in this way they revolve and take turns firing in a constant stream. (Quoted in Andrade 2016: 155)

Cheng advocated volley-shooting for use in Ming armies and also

A Ming Dynasty (1368–1644) crossbowman in action. Crossbowmen like this are often depicted in rotating ranks of three – spanning, advancing and shooting. The lath is inexpensively made from bound bamboo strips and it is spanned by hand, using the carrying lanyard as a stirrup. Simplicity of both manufacture and operation made it ideally suited for use by massed troops. Although use of the crossbow had begun to decline for the main army at this period, it was still used in great numbers by local auxiliaries. The Ming period saw a divergence of crossbow forms. The bamboo-strip construction method adapted easily to a wide variety of sizes and strengths and working replica great-crossbows of the period have been made using as many as 20 strips of bamboo for the lath. The Miao, a mountain people from Southern China, were also famous for their great-crossbows; in their case fitted with massive wooden laths. Spanned by hand, these took three people to draw the string back, each bracing a foot on the lath. By contrast the standard five-strip bamboo lath, hand-spanned by one man, was relatively weak, its advantage being that it could be deployed in large numbers and shot in volleys. (David Joseph Wright)

that crossbowmen should be trained in the use of either the lance or the sword for close-quarter defence. It must be obvious that drilling troops for volley-shooting is the most useful way to employ massed crossbowmen on the battlefield. Unfortunately, there is a lack of evidence to support such an idea on European battlefields. That is not to say that such tactics were not used; merely that we do not know they were. We know even less of the crossbow's use by Greece and Rome.

THE CROSSBOW IN EUROPE

The crossbow in Europe seems to disappear from the record after the end of the Western Roman Empire in the 5th century AD, not reappearing until sometime in the 10th century. Crossbow use is recorded by the French chronicler Richerus at the siege of Senlis in 949 and again at the siege of Verdun in 984 (Blackmore 1971: 175). It seems unlikely that it would have fallen out of use entirely for 500 years but, perhaps used only by the stealthy hands of poachers, it has left no trace during the intervening time. The earliest archaeological find to date is the remains of an 11th-century crossbow found at Lake Paladru, north-west of Grenoble. It is small (20 inches in length). During the 11th century occasional flickers of the crossbow's existence occur in the record – William of Poitiers (d. 1090) affirms their presence at the battle of Hastings (1066) and William Rufus was killed by a crossbow bolt in 1100. By the early 12th century, however, the crossbow had entered general use as a mainstream battlefield weapon. The first flood of information, from both Arab and Western sources, comes to light during the Crusades to the Holy Land, where it was used by all sides.

Anna Komnene gives a vivid description of how these early crossbows were used: 'this instrument of war has to be stretched by lying almost on one's back; each foot is pressed forcibly against the half circles of the bow and the hands tug at the bow, pulling it with all one's strength towards the body' (Komnene 2009: 282).

A reconstruction of a wooden crossbow by Andreas Bichler representing a type from c.1200. The lath is made of ash with a backing layer of sinew. It has a draw-weight of around 80lb. For all the many improvements that were made to crossbows over the centuries – composite laths, steel laths and various spanning devices – the simple wooden bow was the one that was the most used in warfare. This example is fitted with a stirrup to assist with spanning. Before the stirrup was introduced at some point in the late 12th century, however, crossbows otherwise identical to this had to be spanned by the crossbowman, or a companion loader, sitting on the ground and bracing the lath against his feet while he pulled back with both hands. This, without the stirrup, is the type of bow that Richard I's *ballestriarii* would have used during the English king's campaigns in the Holy Land. (Photograph: Andreas Bichler)

44

Men of the crossbow

The troubadour Ambroise, who gave a poetic account of the Third Crusade (1189–92), wrote after the battle of Arsuf (1191), 'That day our excellent crossbowmen fought nobly and did service yeoman' (quoted in Strickland & Hardy 2005: 106). Arsuf was one of several victories for Richard I of England (r. 1189–99), as commander of the Frankish forces. He was an ardent proponent of the crossbow. Famously, arriving by ship to raise the siege at Jaffa (1192), he leapt into the surf at the head of his men and waded ashore, shooting his crossbow as he did so. Richard relied heavily on specialist crossbowmen, *ballestriarii*, from Genoa and Pisa for his victories in the Holy Land. For his subsequent campaigns in France, he imported recruits from Syria, including Peter de Tanentonne and Martin of Nazareth and their companies of crossbowmen (Strickland & Hardy 2005: 115). It seems likely that this contingent were among the first to bring the composite bow to Europe. In 1205, Peter the Saracen was sent to Northampton to make and repair crossbows at a wage of 6d per day. It is probable that he too was a maker of the new-fangled composite laths. Sixpence was also the daily wage for 'Turpin the *arbilistarius*' sent on Prince John's Irish campaign of 1184–85; Strickland suggests he may be the same Turpin who received a land grant in France from Richard I in 1190 (Strickland & Hardy 2005: 115). It was certainly common for crossbowmen to achieve elevated status. William Le Breton recounted that Richard's one-time friend and later bitter rival Philip II Augustus, king of France (r. 1180–1222), rewarded his crossbowmen handsomely and that he 'enriched them with manors, goods and money' (quoted in Strickland & Hardy 2005: 115). Richard's younger brother John (r. 1199–1216) accorded his crossbowmen similar value; he endowed them with lands and pensions and ranked them immediately after the knights. Higher-ranking crossbowmen in service on his campaign in Normandy (1202–04) received an astonishing 4s per day (Powicke 1960: 225).

When the crusading baton passed to other European monarchs they too placed great store by crossbowmen. Some 4,000 crossbowmen served on the Fifth Crusade (1217–21) and Louis IX of France took 5,000 crossbowmen to Egypt during the Seventh Crusade (1248–54). The great Templar castle at Saphet was garrisoned in 1260 with 50 knights and 300 crossbowmen (Strickland & Hardy 2005: 114). Mercenary crossbowmen were in constant demand for European armies throughout the medieval period. In 1215 both mercenaries and crossbowmen featured in the provisions of Magna Carta imposed on King John, 'And immediately after concluding peace we will remove alien knights, crossbowmen, serjeants and mercenary soldiers' (quoted in Carpenter 1996: 11).

Such conditions related to the limitation of royal martial power and John's reliance on foreign mercenaries rather than irrational prejudice against the weapon itself. Notwithstanding the curtailments of Magna Carta, Henry III of England (r. 1216–72) and his regent William Marshall continued to employ foreign crossbowmen in the service of the English crown, favouring recruits from Gascony. Others were recruited from Anjou, Poitou, Flanders, Brittany, Spain and Portugal, as well from several Italian city-states. They were all professional soldiers, worthy of their high reputation. Henry III maintained a retinue of 20 crossbowmen for his personal protection and he considered the crossbow to be of such importance that, in 1255, he instructed his sheriffs to ensure that all *cruce-signati* (those pledged to go on crusade) practised with it on a regular basis (Tyerman 1988: 168).

Henry III's son, Edward I (r. 1272–1307) deployed an elite force of Gascon crossbowmen in his Welsh campaign of 1282–83 (Strickland & Hardy 2005: 114). Although Edward I recruited unprecedented numbers of longbowmen for his Scottish campaigns, he did not neglect the crossbow. He sent significant numbers of crossbowmen to Scotland and, in 1295, ordered London to send 500 crossbowmen for the defence of the coast. Also in 1295 was the battle of Maes Moydog; an engagement in which Edward I's close friend, William de Beauchamp, Earl of Warwick, triumphed over Welsh forces. He used a combination of archers and crossbowmen, together with his cavalry, to rout the army of Madog ap Llywelyn. Notably, he placed one crossbowman in between every two cavalrymen (Bradbury 1985: 84). By using combined forces Warwick was able to break the Welsh squares of spearmen. Standing just a short way off, cavalry could be quick to exploit the gaps in the line created by bolts thudding into the lightly armoured infantry.

By the 13th century, feudal tenure, that is holding land in exchange for service, extended to crossbowmen. John de Cordebof held land in Mendlesham, Suffolk 'by sergeanty of staying with his crossbow in the

Jaffa, 5 August 1192 (opposite)

Having relieved the town of Jaffa after a spectacular amphibious landing, the crusader forces under Richard Coeur de Lion were faced with a major land battle against Saladin's larger army. Saladin's forces consisted of an estimated 7,000 light cavalry, many of whom were horse-archers. Richard's forces numbered just 50–60 knights and around 2,000 infantry. A large proportion of these were Genoese and Pisan crossbowmen; the remainder were spearmen.

The spearmen were drawn up in defensive formation, kneeling and with the butts of their spears dug in to present a glinting porcupine of spearheads at the height of a horse's chest. More than half the knights dismounted to command sections of this shield-wall and to hold the men steady. Behind and in between the spearmen were the crossbowmen. They worked in pairs – a loader and a shooter – so as to maintain a constant barrage of bolts against the enemy. Hammered into the rocky ground in front of them was a field of iron tent-pegs, causing certain crippling injury to any horse that stepped on them. It is an inviolable rule of military archery that archers, especially crossbowmen, can only operate successfully in well-defended positions.

Saladin's horsemen were unable to close and wheeled about in successive attacks. Each time the efforts of his horse-archers were outmatched by Richard's crossbowmen, who relentlessly hauled back their strings to send bolt after bolt thudding into the vulnerable cavalry. Lancers and swordsmen could not get within arm's reach.

After much slaughter, Saladin's forces held back and Richard led a counter-attack with his crossbowmen at the head of the line, shooting as they advanced. The crusaders had fewer than ten mounted men and yet Saladin's mighty army of horsemen was driven from the field. It was a remarkable victory for the crossbow and the final battle of the Third Crusade (1189–92).

army for forty days at his own cost', and William le Areblaster held four carucates (about 120 acres) 'by crossbow service and doing guard at York castle in time of war for forty days at his own cost, and if longer at the king's cost, and conducting the king's treasure through the country at the king's cost' (quoted in Bradbury 1985: 79). Forty days was the standard term for feudal service. After that the crown had to raise cash to pay its armies, as it did also when recruiting for foreign adventures. Feudal service was only for duties at home.

Domestic recruitment of crossbowmen continued long after the ascendancy of the longbow. In November 1314, a few months after the English defeat at Bannockburn, the north of England was deemed to be in peril. Consequently the cities of York, Lincoln, Northampton and London were ordered to supply crossbowmen 'armed with aketons [padded coats], coats of mail or bascinets of plate at the king's expense' (Powicke 1962: 142). The requirement for them to turn out as well-armoured infantry suggests that they could be expected to make a stand in the field, as well as to garrison towns and castles.

Although it is difficult to evaluate the worth of rates of pay, especially as they occur in changing economies from one period to another, we can discern the relative value of crossbowmen compared to other troops. It is universally the case that crossbowmen were paid well and at a higher rate than longbowmen. The economics of fielding large contingents of longbowmen was one of the reasons they were so beloved of impoverished English kings. In the mid-14th century, at a time when a longbow archer received 3d per day and a mounted (longbow) archer received 6d a day, a crossbowman was paid 8d per day – the same as a man-at-arms on foot (Bell, Curry, King & Simpkin 2013: 190). Although sailors and garrison troops could be provided with crossbows by the crown, the soldier on campaign was more likely to own his own weapon. A significant capital investment was required to command these higher wages.

According to a 1381 inventory of his goods, a London grocer, one Richard Toky, owned not only a crossbow but also four hand-bows, arrows, bolts and armour (Bradbury 1985: 175). He may have possessed both his crossbow and his hand-bows for hunting, but it is equally possible that he owned them because he boosted his income occasionally by short-term enlistments in military campaigns; sometimes as an archer and sometimes as a crossbowmen. It all depended on what the job market at the time required.

Crossbowmen in the 15th century

The universities of Southampton and Reading have produced an online resource (http://www.medievalsoldier.org) that provides a searchable database, derived from muster rolls and counter rolls, of medieval soldiery serving in late-medieval English armies. A search for crossbowmen revealed the following breakdown of postings between 1415 and 1450.

After the English victory at Agincourt (1415), many French towns came under English occupation and by far the majority of crossbowmen on the rolls – 55 per cent – were recruited for garrison duty. Urban defences were a crossbowman's main workplace. Great towns such as Rouen even gave the specific patrol location – town, castle or gates. In the case of Poissy, it was the bridge that required guarding. A further 7 per cent were posted on city watch with all the policing duties that implied. Just over 5 per cent served in either the personal retinue of a knight or were on escort duty for great nobles. Roughly 13 per cent were listed as rendering field service for a siege and 3 per cent did not have their duties recorded.

Naval service accounted for the remaining 17 per cent. This was divided between 'naval expeditions', 'keeping of the sea' and 'naval sieges'. Port towns were prime targets for attacks by crossbowmen aboard ships.

Further analysis by the authors of this study has demonstrated that many soldiers served as different troop types over time (Bell, Curry, King & Simpkin 2013: 191). For instance, Raymond de Lor served as a gunner in 1442, but did duty as a crossbowman at Rouen in 1446. He also served as an archer on two other occasions. Similarly, one John Paskyn began his military career as an archer in the retinue of Lord Willoughby and then served as a crossbowman under Sir John Fastolf before returning to Lord Willoughby's ranks as a man-at-arms. In English armies, at least, versatility was a key asset, with men taking up the crossbow when that was the weapon most apt for the mission. Whether a man's primary expertise was as an archer, a halberdier or a gunner, the crossbow's ease of use made it available to anyone seeking military employment.

Nevertheless, the profession of crossbowman was pursued more earnestly and more single-mindedly by troops from mainland Europe, where the weapon enjoyed a higher status. Doubtless the levels of proficiency – accuracy and speed – of 'career' crossbowmen exceeded the capabilities of more occasional recruits. The English army rolls are populated conspicuously with crossbowmen from Portugal, Genoa and Flanders as well as those from home.

Mounted crossbowmen

In exchange for his sergeantry (land grant for feudal service), Henry I (r. 1100–35) obliged Gerard Tusard 'to find one Archer on horseback for the King's service, also a crossbow for him to shoot with, and to maintain him 40 days in the King's army at his own cost, whenever the King went into Wales' (THCN: 326). Here the term 'Archer on horseback' is clearly used to mean a mounted crossbowman. Mounted crossbowmen could be deployed more speedily than infantry. They could be sent quickly to garrison a captured stronghold, they could patrol with a law-and-order function and they could provide flank protection to travelling retinues.

Many thousands of mounted crossbowmen were recruited by crusading armies, providing an essential screening function to the columns of knights that were vulnerable to the harassing attacks of horse-archers and light infantry. However, like mounted (longbow) archers these were dragoon troops. Dismounting for battle was the defining characteristic of

Shooting the crossbow on horseback

The Museum of the Han Dynasty (206 BC–AD 220) in Xuzhou, China, contains a carved stone image of a horseman spanning his crossbow (he also has a severed head hanging from the saddle) and the Nan Yang museum has a painting of a Han Dynasty horseman, carrying his crossbow over his shoulder, riding as an escort to a dignitary being driven in a chariot. To date these are the earliest known references to the crossbow being used from horseback.

In Arrian's *Ars Tactica*, a treatise on Roman cavalry tactics written in about AD 136, there is mention of 'missiles shot not from a bow but from a machine' (quoted in Hyland 1993: 76). Given that the context is for this 'machine' to be operated on horseback, it seems most probable that Arrian is referring to the *arcuballista* – the Roman crossbow. It is listed among other mounted weapon skills to be performed at the gallop. Unfortunately, no evidence exists elsewhere to indicate the prevalence of this use. Curiously, perhaps the earliest depiction of the crossbow during the medieval period is of a rider, at full gallop, carrying a spanned crossbow in one hand. It is remarkably similar in style to the *arcuballista* type. This image, a detail from a Catalan manuscript, *The Four Horsemen of the Apocalypse*, now in the Cathedral Library, Burgo de Osma, Spain, dates to 1086. Even so, crossbow cavalry, as distinct from dragoon-style mounted crossbowmen, remain elusive in the historical record, despite

A Mamluk military treatise, the *Kitāb al-mahzūn ğāmiʿ al-funūn* (*c.*1470), shows a crossbowman shooting his weapon at full gallop. Note the extremely long tiller, couched under the arm in the manner of a lance and giving greater stability and counterbalance to the crossbow in motion. Long tillers are also seen in contemporary depictions of Arab infantry crossbowmen. A long tiller allows for the trigger lever to be set further back – note the position of the trigger hand – which in turn allows for the nut to be set further back, delivering a longer power-stroke. The rider retains the reins in his left hand while shooting. There is no indication of a spanning aid other than a stirrup, so the bow was presumably of relatively light draw-weight. It is a simple matter to hand-span from the saddle using a stirrup crossbow, given a bow of manageable power. (Bibliothèque nationale de France, Paris)

numerous depictions of crossbowmen shooting from their horses in the hunting field throughout the medieval period.

It is certainly possible to shoot a crossbow from horseback. I have done so, both stationary and at full gallop. The trick, when in motion, is to keep the bolt in place by holding its tail with the tip of your thumb over the nut – the tail protrudes a fraction above the claw of the nut and a light pressure is all that is required. An alternative method is to use a bolt-retaining clip, but this slows loading, undesirable in a military context. The more pressing problem is the business of spanning.

Emperor Maximilian I (r. 1493–1519) was especially keen on hunting dangerous game with the crossbow from horseback. For such risky undertakings a powerful bow was required and for heavy draw-weight bows, a cranequin was the only option for the mounted man. Hung from either the saddle or the belt, the cranequin was elementary for a rider to manage provided that the horse stood reasonably still. Many examples in 15th- and 16th-century art show cranequins being used by hunters on horseback. For martial purposes, however, the cranequin was frustratingly slow. Lighter to carry and quicker to use, albeit less powerful, was the goat's foot lever or gaffle.

Asserting his preference for crossbows over pistols for mounted men – pistoliers were prone to spill the powder when trying to load their pieces on a fidgety horse – Sir John Smythe, writing in 1590, recommended that mounted arbalists be equipped with gaffles: 'For all the crossbowers on horseback … I would they should have crossbows of two pound and a half of the best sort, with crooked gaffles hanging at their strong girdles after the manner of Germany, that they might on horseback bend their crossbows the more easily and readily, with four-and-twenty quarrels in a case' (Smythe 1964: 113).

Whether his 'two pound and a half' was an error of penmanship or a shorthand expression of the day, it seems reasonable to interpret it as a draw-weight of 250lb, which would be consistent with using a gaffle. He goes on to say that he advises his crossbowmen be mounted upon 'good cold geldings' (Smythe 1964: 113). That is to say horses of a very steady (cold-blood) temperament, suited for transport and for the business of spanning and shooting a crossbow but not for the dash of the battlefield. The artist Albrecht Dürer (1471–1528) shows a mercenary soldier armed with a crossbow on just such a horse. Perhaps in compensation for his workaday mount, the soldier wears puff and slash clothing over his breastplate and displays a crossbow bolt in his feathered bonnet for additional debonair dash. Images of similar – though less ostentatiously dressed – troops are common in numerous *Hausbücher*. *Hausbücher* (housebooks), popular in German lands during the 15th century, were books of drawings that recorded everyday life, especially military retinues. They often depict mounted crossbowmen forming part of a lance – a military unit of the 14th and 15th centuries, comprising a small band of differing troop types in support of a knight. Among them were halberdiers, archers and, usually, a crossbowman. All were mounted to travel together, though most fought dismounted. Mounted crossbowmen in the *Hausbücher* are shown with gaffles, but these did not appear until the 14th century. What, then, of Gerard Tusard in the early 12th century – how might he have spanned his bow in the saddle?

A clue comes from a Mamluk manuscript. Taybughā describes using the belt-and-claw method from horseback:

> The drawing-claw should have two hooks. What the archer does is slip the drawing-strap over his left shoulder … placing the claw beneath his right armpit close to the nipple. When he wishes to shoot he takes the reins in his left hand and the bow in his right and sets the string in the hooks, keeping the stock right in between them. He then bends forward in a stooping position until the front half of his right foot is in the stirrup [of the crossbow]. The archer now stands in his stirrups [of the saddle], as he draws the string at its centre point until it catches in the nut … This done, he bends over forward, removes his foot from the bow and lifting the crossbow off the hook, transfers it to his left hand and holds it along with his reins. He nocks his bolts with his right hand and shoots in the usual way to destroy the enemy. (Latham & Paterson 1970: 85–86)

With this, Taybughā offers a system that could be utilized from the back of a galloping horse. Those who doubt the possibility of spanning by this method at speed should consider that some Ottoman archery treatises describe archers unstringing and then restringing their powerful composite bows from the saddle at the gallop (Loades 2016: 46); by comparison, bending the crossbow was a lesser feat. More importantly, Taybughā makes it clear that the intended use for his mounted spanning method was in battle. He further notes that even a 'slightly-built archer' can shoot a crossbow of considerable draw-weight and that it can be used 'after only a few days practice' (Latham & Paterson 1970: 85–86).

Smythe reinforces the idea that crossbowmen should be able to both shoot and span their weapon on a moving horse: 'Both archers and crossbowers, I would have to be well practiced that they might know how to discharge their arrows and quarrels galloping along the hand and in all other motions of their horses, and the crossbowers to bend again with great readiness' (Smythe 1964: 114). Note that the phrase 'hand-gallop' remains in use today and denotes a speed faster than a canter, though not quite a flat-out gallop. Smythe capped this advocacy with 'I come to conclude that crossbowers on horseback used by many foreign nations of great antiquity … do far exceed and excel all weapons of fire on horseback' (Smythe 1964: 115). It is important to note that Smythe was not necessarily observing contemporary practice, rather suggesting what he thought would be improvements to it.

A mounted crossbowman shooting over his shoulder, from Hans Talhoffer's 1459 *Fechtbuch* (Ms. Thott 290.2⁰), illustrated by Michel Rotwyler. This technique permits a far more direct shot at a pursuer than would be possible from turning in the saddle and also allows the rider to manage his reins. Both this and a second image of a mounted crossbowman in the manuscript portray the combatants in civilian dress, suggesting that this was one of the many weapon configurations for the judicial combats popular in German lands at the time. In his 1467 *Fechtbuch*, Talhoffer shows the mounted crossbowman pitted against a mounted man with a heavy lance. He illustrates how, having shot his bolt at the lancer, the crossbowman may use his weapon to parry and lift the oncoming lance to one side. (Hans Talhoffer/Wikimedia/Public Domain)

This manuscript illustration from *c.*1340 (Klosterneuburger Evangelienwerk, Stadtbibliothek Schaffhausen, Gen. 8., fol. 303v) is an allegorical scene that cannot be taken literally. Even so, the presence of the mounted crossbowman, shooting from the saddle, is noteworthy. (Image courtesy of Stadtbibliothek Schaffhausen)

mounted archers, in contradistinction to horse-archers who shot from the saddle at the gallop. Mounted crossbowmen operated in a similar way to mounted archers, dismounting to fight, though it is probable that, on occasion, they also shot their bows from the saddle.

Mounted crossbowmen were remunerated handsomely. In the 12th century, those in the pay of Philip II Augustus, king of France (r. 1180–1222) received 48–54d per day compared to the 12–18d paid to the infantry crossbowman (Strickland & Hardy 2005: 115). This variation in pay may indicate not only rank according to experience but also to the number of horses the mounted crossbowmen brought into service. In a unit of 84 mounted crossbowmen in the service of King John of England in 1200, 26 had three horses each, 52 had two horses each and seven had one horse each (Strickland & Hardy 2005: 115). Mounted crossbowmen were especially suitable for escort duty. As late as 1515, at the battle of Marignano, Francis I, king of France (r. 1515–47), had 200 mounted crossbowmen serving as his bodyguard (Payne-Gallwey 1903: 48).

Arbalist armour

Replicas of three types of helmet commonly worn by European crossbowmen. These are known variously as war hats, iron hats, kettle hats and *chapeaux de fer*. Two examples – one dating from the 13th century (**1**) and the other from the 14th century (**2**) – are based on wall paintings in Austria, while an example from the 15th century (**3**) is modelled on types seen in Burgundian art. Crossbowmen were always extremely well armoured, and – as demonstrated by (**3**) – they could sometimes be quite resplendent. These helmets are all brightly burnished, but it was also common to paint iron hats in the livery colours of the crossbowman's company. Painted armour was in regular use during the 12th and 13th centuries, serving not only as an identifier but also as a protection against rust. In addition to his crossbow and his war hat, the crossbowman had to provide serviceable armour. In earlier periods this consisted of a stout aketon (padded coat) and mail. By the second half of the 15th century he might also have had to provide plate armour. It is an advantage of the crossbow that it can be operated by a fully armoured man. Crossbowmen were heavy infantry and the expense of their equipment was one of the reasons they could command relatively high wages. Broad-brimmed helmets such as these were a distinctive element of the crossbowman's accoutrements. The crossbowman could shoot his weapon in such headgear without obstruction, something that would not have been possible for the longbowman. The broad brim gave protection to the face and throat when bending over to span and also when shooting the crossbow with the head tilted slightly downwards, sighting along the tiller. War hats were well suited to siege operations, an aspect of warfare in which crossbowmen excelled. When approaching walls, they shielded against stones and missiles raining down from above. (**1** and **2**: Andreas Bichler; **3**: Jason Daub)

THE CROSSBOW IN THE SIEGE

There can be little doubt that, whatever its battlefield successes, the crossbow's most natural habitat was on the ramparts, whether they be town wall or castle. Fortifications gave security to the time-consuming business of spanning and the crossbowman was only briefly vulnerable for the split second his shot was taken. The period of the crossbow's ascendancy coincided with the evolution of the medieval castle; each had a symbiotic relationship with the other.

In his chronicle *Flores Historiarum*, Roger of Wendover (d. 1236) tells of the fate of many crossbowmen who fought on the losing side at the siege of Rochester Castle in 1215. The castle had been held against King John by a force of rebel barons, but after a protracted siege, the royal forces prevailed: 'All the soldiers, except the crossbowmen, he gave up to his own soldiers to be ransomed; and some of the crossbowmen, who had slain many of his knights and soldiers during the siege, he ordered to be hung' (Wendover 1849: 339). Such retribution, singling out crossbowmen for the ultimate penalty, underlines both the importance and the effectiveness of crossbowmen in a defended position. In later centuries Henry V (r. 1413–22) made a similar exception at the siege of Rouen (1419). Despite offering clemency to the majority of the defenders, he singled out Alain Blanchard, the leader of the crossbowmen, for execution (Bradbury 1985: 307).

Matthew Paris (*c.*1200–59) added a marginal note in his chronicle telling the story of a crossbowman in the service of William of Alberney. They had seen King John riding to inspect the siege defences and the crossbowman enquired of his master whether or not he should shoot. Alberney replied, 'No, no; far be it for us villein, to cause the death of the Lord's anointed' (Wendover 1849: 339). Given the fate of John's elder brother, this is possibly a romantic fiction intended to convey a reassuring sense of divine order at a time of turmoil. Nevertheless, it speaks to the use of the crossbow as a fearsome sniper's weapon.

Crossbowmen again played a central role at the siege of Lincoln (1217). Prince Louis (1187–1226), later King Louis VIII of France (r. 1223–26), had landed in England and claimed the English crown. He had support from English barons and had laid siege to Lincoln Castle. William Marshall, regent to the young King Henry III, assembled an army consisting of, among others, 406 knights and 317 crossbowmen. They marched on Lincoln to raise the siege. Roger of Wendover tells us that 'The crossbowmen all the time kept in advance of the army' (Wendover 1849: 393). This insight into march formation hints that, in the event of encountering the enemy, the crossbowmen would create a forward screen, holding ground while the rest of the army organized. Once efforts to raise the siege were under way, crossbowmen were again in the vanguard:

> Falkes de Breaute entered the castle with the company of troops under his command, and with the crossbowmen, and stationed them on the roofs of the buildings and on the ramparts, whence they discharged their deadly weapons against the chargers of the barons, levelling horses and riders together to the earth … At length, by means of the

crossbowmen, by whose skill the horses of the barons were mown down and killed like pigs, the party of the barons was greatly weakened. (Wendover 1849: 394–95)

When shooting a crossbow in depression – that is, tilting it downwards to aim – the same procedure as shooting it from horseback applied. In order to prevent the bolt from slipping off, it was kept in place by applying a light pressure on its tail with the thumb. Crossbows were not only suitable for shooting down at attackers and up at defenders; they were also ideal for use on belfries (mobile siege towers). Although belfries could be, and were, employed to send troops over the walls, their principal function was to give cover to workings at ground level. These might be either a ram or mining operations. Crossbowmen on the upper levels were well positioned to keep defenders at bay; enemy troops who might otherwise be leaning over the ramparts to drop stones or shoot down with crossbows. Belfries, enormous and perilously top-heavy structures on wheels, were manoeuvred into position with ponderous progress. One account from the Second Crusade (1147–49) describes a tower moving just 90 feet in one day (Bradbury 1985: 249). Such a sluggish advance required good missile defences against those who would rush to topple it.

Crossbows were sometimes used by spies to send intelligence messages to the enemy. During the siege of Rhodes in 1522, Apella Renata shot a message to the besieging Turks with his crossbow. He was hanged and quartered. Blasco Diaz was put to the rack for a similar use of his crossbow. Unable to walk, he had to be carried to his execution (Bradbury 1985: 317).

The late-medieval author Christine de Pizan (1364–1430) recorded detailed lists of the armaments necessary to defend a castle or town against a siege. Although many of her recommendations were copied from the pages of a 5th-century Roman writer on military matters – Vegetius – her references to gunpowder weapons and to various types of crossbow are unmistakably contemporary. Notwithstanding that she does not mention the size of the place to be defended, her emphasis on a wide range of crossbow types is revealing. She recommended 'three large crossbows on wheels, provided with the necessary arrows ... twenty-four good crossbows well equipped, six others on wooden bases ... twelve score

Crossbowmen manning the hoarding (opposite)

Crossbowmen in action during the siege of a castle, c.1200. Castle ramparts and towers – as well as some town walls – were augmented by a wooden gallery, called a hoarding. This provided a platform overhanging the walls. Apertures in the floor could be used to drop stones onto the heads of attackers trying to work at the base of the walls with picks or to ascend with ladders. The low ceiling and confined conditions made the hoarding especially suitable for use by crossbowmen, who could move quickly around the walls to any trouble-spot that required manning. Here the crossbowmen work in teams of two, so that while one is shooting, the other is spanning his weapon. Both wooden-lathed and composite-lathed crossbows are in use and both are spanned by the belt-and-claw method.

crossbows with hooks ... twelve machines for bending crossbows' (Pizan 1999: 111). The twelve score (240) crossbows with hooks were obviously belt-and-claw bows, signalling the importance of such weapons in great number. The three large crossbows on wheels and the six on wooden bases must surely have been great-crossbows, though the precise nature of the 24 'good crossbows' is uncertain. The 'twelve machines for bending crossbows' could refer to large spanning stands or perhaps windlasses. It may be that these were for the 24 'good crossbows', indicating two bows for each of the 'machines'. There is a great deal of sense in having one man spanning one bow while his fellow shoots the other.

Crossbows being shot downwards from towers and ramparts have a clear range advantage compared to those of the besiegers, who are shooting upwards. Even so, the standard, hand-held crossbow should be considered a relatively short-range weapon, most effective at distances less than 100 yards and even more effective at very close range. When the ladders are against the walls and the ramparts are at the gate, when the belfry trundles into range or when men smash through the hoardings and onto the wall-walks, then the crossbowmen of the garrison must run to their posts, hurry up winding stairs and along narrow walkways, to stem the tide of an enemy attack. Then their portable weapons can perform much service. For most of the long hours, days and weeks of a siege, however, the enemy busies himself with activities beyond ordinary range. To harass him here the garrison must possess great-crossbows.

Great-crossbows

Great-crossbows were most usually placed on the top of towers, partly in order to give them greater range and partly because, on a tower, they could be turned to cover more angles than would be possible in an embrasure. Some castles, such as Krak des Chevaliers in Syria, did feature embrasures large enough to accommodate a great-crossbow on a spanning bench, but these are the exceptions to the rule. The primary task of a great-crossbow was to be able to strike at distant targets and this was better accomplished from a position of height. This also made it less vulnerable to counter-attack. It is sometimes difficult to discern from the records when a great-crossbow is being referred to, particularly where the only clue is that it is spanned by a 'windlass'. Not all crossbows spanned by a windlass were great-crossbows, but the context, including cost and quantity, can be a useful indicator.

In 1209, during the Albigensian Crusade (1209–29), Simon de Montfort deployed 'balestas tornessas' on the tower of the Château Narbonnais so that he could shoot over the walls of the town of Toulouse, which were no more than 100 yards away. During the *reconquista* of the Balearic Isles, James the Conqueror, King of Aragon (r. 1213–76), sent for a powerful 'windlass crossbow' at the siege of Majorca in 1229. He requested it specifically for use against the enemy's counter-mine operations. One imagines it, set on a low bench, at the opening where the enemy tunnel intercepted James' workings. Even if a suicide squad of men had been coerced to lead the attack, their certain deaths would have

The pavise

Crossbows took time to span and, on the battlefield, crossbowmen were immensely vulnerable to the missiles of the enemy. During the 14th century a type of very large shield, called a pavise, was developed. It is believed to have originated in Pavia, one of many Italian city-states renowned for the prowess of its crossbowmen. This Pavian shield gave protection to a kneeling or crouching man while he was spanning his crossbow. Exposure was minimal when he levelled his weapon above the top edge to shoot. A distinctive feature of pavise design was a raised central panel. The corrugated shape provided rigidity to the design, thus allowing lightweight materials to be used in its construction. It also shelved slightly at the top edge to create a rest for the crossbow when shooting and provided a recess at the back to allow a prop to be stowed neatly away for carriage. Crossbowmen had to carry their pavises into position on the field, which they did by hoisting them onto their backs with a pair of straps. The gutter of the central ridge bridged the spine, so that the shield sat comfortably. Even so, pavises were too cumbersome for infantry to carry on a long march and too large for mounted crossbowmen to shoulder when on horseback. Pavises were usually transported on the baggage train.

Genoese crossbowmen at the battle of Crécy (1346) were forced onto the field without their pavises by their impatient French paymasters. Their pavises were on a baggage train that had become stalled at the back of the main French army. Once they came into range of the English longbowmen, the Genoese crossbowmen were defenceless and outranged. It is little wonder that they took the prudent military decision to retreat from that position, despite the hot-headed haranguing of their French commanders. There is an old story that they fled because their strings had suffered in the downpour that preceded the battle. It is nonsense. Well-waxed strings are impervious to the effects of damp. Sir Ralph Payne-Gallwey, writing in 1903, claims to have sunk a strung crossbow in a tank of water for a day and a night and observed no difference in the tautness of the string (Payne-Gallwey 1903: 5).

Two views of a replica pavise constructed using narrow-gauge boards of linden (lime). The boards were dowelled and glued together. Linden was a traditional wood for shields because it is both light and strong. Even so, in panel form, it required additional strengthening. A linen canvas, soaked in rabbit-skin glue, was laid over the boards. As it dried, the canvas shrank and so tied all the boards tightly together, enhancing the overall structural strength. The shape of the central ridge created additional rigidity. For decorated pavises like this, several layers of gesso (a mixture of glue and plaster) were applied, smoothed and painted, before being sealed with a shellac varnish. Pavises were often wondrous examples of medieval art and many splendid examples survive. Coats-of-arms of the town and heraldic displays of guild affiliations were common and some, like this example, were also adorned with fine-art paintings worthy of an altarpiece. On the back is a pair of shoulder straps and a handgrip. Traditionally, handgrips were made from a bull's pizzle. (Pavise built and photographed by Alex Kay, Sir John Paston's Household)

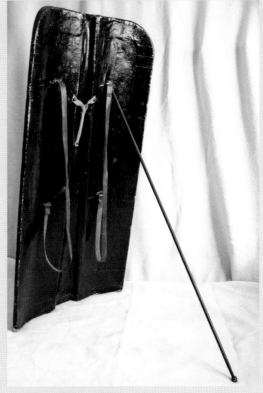

blocked the tunnel long enough for the great-crossbow to be reloaded. It was a considerable deterrent.

Christine de Pizan asserted that six windlass crossbows were required in a town or castle under siege, and 30 to attack one (quoted in Liebel 1998: 38). When attacking a fortification, these valuable machines had to be installed behind good defences. Great-crossbows could not be moved easily if attacked. Whereas the crossbowman in the field relied on his portable pavise, the soldier laying siege required something more substantial – a mantlet. Mantlets were relatively large, freestanding structures that defended against projectiles and provided a solid barrier against marauding sorties. Osier wickerwork was a common construction medium; it was lightweight and adequate against arrows. Wooden mantlets, made with sturdy boards, offered greater protection, but were heavier and more cumbersome to manoeuvre. On occasion both wicker and wooden mantlets were fitted with wheels, affording them some mobility. More elaborate structures, L-shapes for instance, were capable of sheltering several men and a great-crossbow. It all added to the logistics of fielding these larger weapons. In the Black Prince's Spanish campaigns, which culminated at the battle of Nájera in 1367, he took windlass crossbows on 'carts and carriages' (Liebel 1998: 38); they were clearly larger than a man could carry.

Whether employed in open battle or during a siege, great-crossbows had a terrifying ability to target a leader. During the siege of Paris in 1429, Joan of Arc was struck in the thigh by a bolt from a 'hausspied' crossbow; that is a great-crossbow bent on a spanning stand

(Liebel 1998: 42). She recovered from her wounds, suggesting the large bolt only grazed her. No matter how effective great-crossbows could be at picking off individuals, though, there can be little doubt that their most devastating use was as delivery systems for incendiary ammunition. Medieval recipes for incendiary arrows abound and there is some discussion of this in my book *The Longbow* (Loades 2013: 23). Medieval towns were crammed with timber-framed buildings, many with thatched roofs, nested together in a huddle of narrow streets. They were immensely vulnerable to fire. Great-crossbows were able to deliver it with precision.

BOLTS, BOOZE AND BROTHERHOOD

Guilds, companies and fraternities of crossbowmen flourished in parts of mainland Europe throughout the Middle Ages and thereafter, many surviving to the present day. In Flanders and Northern France, in Swiss and German lands and in many Italian city-states, crossbows were elevated almost to a cult status. These shooting societies were founded, in the words of one 15th-century charter, 'for the security, guard and defence' of the towns (Crombie 2016: 21). The Brussels Guild, founded in 1213, has some claim to be the oldest, but since most charters refer to existing custom and practice, many may be older than that. The strata of society that enlisted to be crossbowmen were similar to those for longbow archers – a broad cross-section of tradesmen – although the crossbow guilds also attracted extremely wealthy burghers to their membership and received the patronage of nobles and princes. Crossbow shooting conferred status.

A great-crossbow mounted on a wheeled carriage, appearing in *Das Feuerwerksbuch* of Martin Merz, 1473 (Cgm 599, fol. 35v.) Also illustrated, though not to scale, is an incendiary bolt armed with a single-barbed head. The expense and physical inconvenience of the great-crossbow is rewarded with its greater range and ability to carry a much heavier missile. This can have no larger pay-off than in the delivery of incendiary ammunition, especially when targeting fortifications that have flammable buildings within. The crossbow has the capacity to be adjusted for both elevation and line with calibrated precision and can be wheeled into position easily. At first sight the bow appears to be without a spanning mechanism, but on the previous page of the manuscript there is a depiction of a large cranequin with a square-section lug extending on the underside of the gearbox. Note the square hole on top of the tiller behind the nut; this was clearly intended to receive the lug on the cranequin. (Bayerische Staatsbibliothek München)

Shooting guilds were as much a part of civic society as they were an adjunct to military organization. Often wearing the livery of their patron, all classes of men met, feasted, drank and shot together on an equal footing. Privileges, which included the right to bear arms, tax exemptions and the prospect of making useful social connections, were among the inducements for recruitment. Members of the Saint Sebastian archery guild in Lille were immune from prosecution for accidental death – a great boon to the more festively inclined arbalist. In most societies, membership was for life, which meant that veterans enjoyed both public esteem and the comradeship of their peers after their years of active service. Most importantly, brothers that were wounded or who fell ill might expect financial support from their fellow members.

The requirements of membership were good character, proficiency at shooting and the ownership of a serviceable crossbow. The guild in Lille specified that a new member should have a crossbow worth £3 and 'other arms needed for the exercise of the bow' within six weeks of joining; Bruges also demanded the provision of costly crossbows valued at £3; whereas in Arras, a 16s crossbow was deemed good enough (Crombie 2016: 65). This cost discrepancy may relate not only to the quality of the bow but also to the 'other arms needed'. A powerful bow requiring the adjunct of an expensive cranequin would clearly cost a lot more than a wooden-lathed bow that could be spanned with a belt-and-claw. For instance, in 1452, a yew crossbow was purchased by the aldermen of Compiègne for a mere 12s. 'A suitable bow' is all that was required for the crossbowmen of Douai in 1383, but in 1499, it was indicated that they had the choice between one with a wood lath or one with a metal lath (Crombie 2016: 65).

As well as providing their weapons, novitiates had to make cash payments to enter a guild or fraternity. The 1442 charter for the Lille guild required them to pay '24 shillings for the profit of the guild' and '12 shillings for drinking in a recreational assembly on the day of their entry'. A further 12s had to be deposited 'which will cover drinking for the confreres who carry the body' as an essential funeral expense (quoted in Crombie 2016: 65–66).

Aside from initial membership dues, shooting fraternities were funded from the town's coffers and in addition to an annual grant of money, there was also an annual grant of wine. Some shooting societies, particularly those in Burgundian lands, included longbow archers as well as crossbowmen and the wine grants give an insight into the hierarchies involved. The town accounts for Lille record that in 1437, the greater crossbowmen received '18 lots of wine' (roughly 8 gallons) and the lesser crossbowmen received '12 lots of wine'. By contrast the greater archers received '12 lots' and the lesser archers '9 lots' (Crombie 206: 129). Clearly, crossbowmen were considered to be of higher status.

As mercantile towns prospered during the Middle Ages, the more they attended to their own security with town walls. Imposing walls were embodiments of civic pride and identity. In a similar fashion the

Detail from a Book of Hours *c.*1530 (ms. II 158, fol. 11v), attributed to Simon Bening. Here, members of a crossbow fraternity gather at their shooting ground. The shooters wear a sumptuous livery, tailored from an abundance of expensive cloth, proclaiming the status of both their town and their guild. A gentleman of great importance watches them, together with other wealthy burghers. Windlasses are required to span the powerful bows and a servant is shown acting as a loader. Such immensely stout laths can only be of composite construction. It is of note that they are bound with security cords, in the manner of steel laths. In this case the bindings would help to prevent the horn delaminating from the sinew, a considerable risk with such short and powerful laths in such an acute arc. The small brick edifice with the grille is for the protection of a scorer. To the left of the picture is one of the target houses. Targets were situated at each end of the range, so that when the shooters had shot one way they would walk to the targets and then turn and shoot the other way. There would be a second scorer's shelter at the opposite end. He would either call out the hits or signal them with a flag.

guardians of these walls, the crossbow societies, became representatives of the town's image. Being properly attired was of importance. Shooting guilds in Flanders, a cloth-producing region, were granted generous amounts of cloth by the town so that the guildsmen could dress in extravagant finery. German guilds were thriftier, bestowing only a grant of trousers or money for trousers (*Hosengeld*). As a further enhancement to a town's prestige, the crossbow guilds of Europe provided impressive spectacle. Shooting competitions were held on a grand scale, with invitations sent far and wide. A great deal of emphasis was placed on procession and theatrical tableaux. In typical form the 1498 invitation to the Ghent contests included the phrase 'the noble game of the crossbow (which) is above and before all other games in morality and nobility' (quoted in Crombie 2016: 178). How attitudes had changed since the papal injunctions of the 11th century.

Well-groomed, permanent shooting grounds were the venues for weekly shooting practice, but the town square was the more usual location for

Replica coronel-headed bolts and box, made by Andreas Bichler. This type of bolt was also used for small game, for the popinjay and for other shooting games. The fellows of European crossbow fraternities carried their prized bolts in decorated boxes that were also emblazoned with heraldic emblems. Competition bolts would be finely tuned, weighted and balanced, for a particular crossbow. Individual bolts were identifiable at a contest because the shooter would write his name onto the shaft with a quill pen. (Photograph: Andreas Bichler)

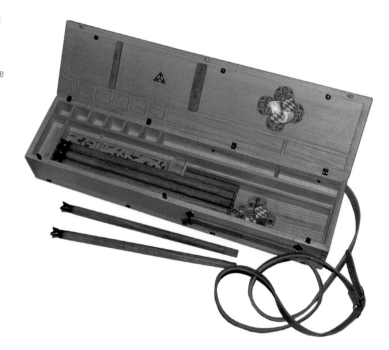

invitational matches in which regional towns assembled to compete, sometimes for as long as a month. For the annual popinjay shoots, a tall mast was erected and wooden birds were placed on transverse spars. These were shot at with heavy blunts in the hope of dislodging them from their high perches. It is my belief that the popinjay began as a practice for naval warfare (Loades 2013: 34). For crossbow shooters masts of tremendous height, 90 feet and greater, were employed. The majority of the matches,

Some examples of common fletching materials for crossbow bolts: feather (**1**), leather (**2**) and parchment (**3**). Old manuscript parchment was frequently cut up and recycled for this purpose. A shallow groove was scored into the shaft in order to receive the base of the fletching. Here, the feather-fletched example uses goose feather, which was the most usual type used. Around 1355, however, the Tower Armoury specified an issue of nearly 1,920 quarrels fletched with hawk feathers (Richardson 2016: 151). (Kim Hawkins)

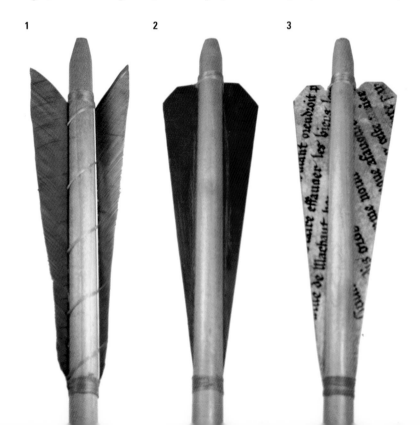

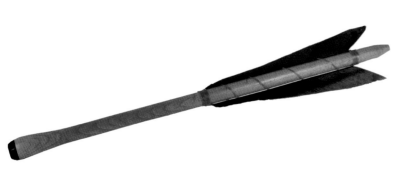

however, were at targets horizontal to the shooters. Lots were drawn to decide who would shoot first. In Tournai in 1455, according to guild records, the shooting order was announced with intricate fanfare:

> A portable meadow had been installed in the town hall. Complete with bushes and flowers made from wax, and in the meadow stood wax female figures representing the companies in attendance. To the heads of these female figures were attached missals bearing the names of the cities and towns which had sent companies to the contests. A beautiful young girl dressed in a bright red tunic embroidered with the emblem of the Tournai crossbowmen stood beside the meadow. The girl held a little rod in her hand which she used to touch each of the wax figures in turn. (Quoted in Crombie 2016: 214)

Such splendour was eclipsed in 1498 with the Antwerp contingent's entrance to the Ghent games. This included over 1,300 people, 50 pageant carts and an elephant (it is uncertain whether this was a live elephant or a wooden one pulled by ropes). At the same event Oudenarde's entrance involved 130 wagons, trumpeters, fair maidens and a procession of horses. Philip the Fair as Duke of Burgundy (r. 1482–1506) led the contingent from Bruges and on another occasion Anthony, the Great Bastard of Burgundy led the contingent from Lille. These were very grand occasions.

The importance of crossbow shooting was also acknowledged in Tudor England. In 1537, Henry VIII (r. 1509–47) granted a charter to the 'Fraternity or Guild of Artillery of Longbows, Crossbows and Handguns'. This became subsequently the Honourable Artillery Company, now recognized as

A replica of a crossbow blunt with a horn cap. Blunts were chiefly employed in shooting games such as the popinjay. They were also used for hunting smaller animals, especially waterfowl. Unlike metal-headed bolts, blunts did not sink and could be retrieved by a dog. In 1576 Elizabeth I's physician John Keys, who adopted the fashionable affectation of Latinizing his name to Johannes Caius, wrote a book on dogs – *Of Englishe Dogges*. In the chapter on water spaniels he notes that 'we use them also to bring us our boultes and our arrowes out of the water' (Caius 2005: 17). Konrad Keyser, in his work *Bellifortis* (1405), proposed insertions into the hollowed-out shafts of blunt bolts that had magical properties. In one formula he recommended axle-grease and the yoke of an egg and in another the heart of a bat. He claimed these would ensure infallible aim (Blackmore 1971: 195). (Kim Hawkins)

A standard medieval quarrel (replica, made by Hector Cole). It has a quartet of faces on each side, making it a slightly flattened octahedron. At the shaft end, the octahedron merges into a cylindrical socket. The four faces nearest the tip are only one-third of the length of the four faces nearest the cylinder of the socket. Quarrels were a universal style of head for the military crossbow. Their distinctive shape ensured immense rigidity, supporting the delivery of energy behind the point. Quarrels were not needle-sharp, but were sufficiently pointed to gain purchase on armour. Two of the outside edges had a relatively sharp cutting profile. Broadheads, while widely used from crossbows in the hunting field, were only used occasionally in warfare. (Kim Hawkins

The King's Quarreler

In determining the cost-effectiveness of any projectile weapon system, the logistics of ammunition procurement are far more important than the cost of the weapons themselves. Quarrels were clearly produced on an industrial scale. Christine de Pizan, in her recommendations for siege preparation, itemized 200,000 quarrels and 1,000 large bolts for provisioning 300 standard crossbows and 30 great-crossbows (Pizan 1999: 121). Between 1344 and 1351, a period when longbow use was at its zenith in English armies, the Tower Armoury issued 103 crossbows and 37,095 quarrels (Richardson 2016: 149). It may be argued that an advantage the crossbow held over the longbow was that quarrels were less complex and therefore less expensive to produce. In either case large stocks had to be held in a nation's arsenals; in time of war supplies could be exhausted rapidly, far more rapidly than it was possible to produce them.

St Briavels Castle in the Royal Forest of Dean, nestled near the English/Welsh border in Gloucestershire, was a major centre for the manufacture of quarrels. At some point during the 1220s Edward I's father, Henry III, sent the smiths William and John de Malemort, together with their fletcher William, to establish a factory there. According to the *Calendar of Liberate Rolls* of Henry III (1226–40) they were paid at the following daily rates: William 7½d, John 6½d and William the fletcher 5½d (Storey 1998: 177). Given that the Crown provided all the materials, together with a house and forge and bellows, it is difficult to ascertain the actual cost of the quarrels. In any event, these were high wages by the standards of the day; a skilled carpenter at this period might only get 2d per day.

It seems probable that William de Malemort was John's father, and that he died shortly after the venture began, because by the 1230s only John de Malemort is mentioned in the records. Between 1241 and 1245, John's atelier produced an astonishing 266,000 quarrels (Storey 1998: 177). St Briavels was only one of a number of manufacturing centres and production on this scale offers an insight into the prevalence of crossbow use in England during the 13th century. By the 1250s John de Malemort was contracted to produce 25,000 quarrels per year for a fee of 25 marks (Storey 1998: 177), which works out at roughly 13d per day for a six-day week. If he had no other costs, then the King's Quarreler was a wealthy man. In 1257 he received double the fee and was expected to produce 50,000 quarrels.

Henry III's son, Edward I, was an even greater patron of his 'great arsenal' at St Briavels. In March 1277, four months before the launch of Edward I's expedition into Wales, there is record of a staggering quantity of quarrels needed to supply his army: 'Order to cause to be made at St. Briavells with all speed 200,000 quarrels, whereof 150,000 shall be for crossbows of one foot and 50,000 for crossbows of two feet, as the king wills that quarrels shall be made and kept there for his use' (CCR Ed I 1277). Clearly, such large-scale production on a tight deadline would be beyond the capacity of one man, and Malemort must have employed a substantial workforce. It may be that he had to pay other workers from his handsome fee. Even orders placed at times of less extravagant military ambition were of a scale to be too much for any individual, such as this requisition in October 1293: 'To John Butetourt, constable of the castle of St. Briavells. Order to cause to be prepared without delay six thousand quarrels, whereof three thousand shall be for two feet [crossbows] and the remainder for one foot, and to deliver them to Richard de Bosco, constable of Corf castle, for the munition of the same' (CCR Ed I 1293).

St Briavels was ideally situated in an area abundant with the raw materials necessary for the manufacture of quarrels. Quarrel

the oldest regiment in the British Army. Its original charter established it for the 'maintenance of the science and feat of shooting in longbows, crossbows and handguns', giving equal status to all three shooting arts.

SUPPLY: BOLTS AND QUARRELS

Although it seems most probable that there were standard sizes for crossbow ammunition (12-inch shafts for the one-foot crossbows and 24-inch shafts for the two-foot or great-crossbows), there were, nevertheless, diverse materials and methods for fletching. Fletching, the attachment of vanes, stops the projectile from turning tail over tip by creating drag at the tail-end. A fletcher fashioned both the shaft and fitted heads required iron ore and this ran in rich seams throughout the area. Copious amounts of charcoal were needed to smelt and forge the ore. Charcoal is a very timber-intensive product and the woodmen of the forest would have had their work cut out supplying the voracious demands of the charcoal-burners. Dense with oak and beech, with their bountiful yield of acorns and mast, the Forest of Dean offered excellent pannage for pigs. Pigs also played a part in the production of quarrel heads – lard was a preferred material for quenching. Quenching is when the red-hot metal is plunged into a cooling medium, in this case lard, in order to cool it at a controlled rate, so affecting the molecular structure and inducing hardness. By quenching in lard, the quarrels were also given some protection against rust. Large batches of bolts required a great deal of fletching and goose feathers seem the most likely material for St Briavels' bolts. Great skeins of geese are drawn to the wetlands of the Severn Estuary and so there was a plentiful, local supply. Numerous fast-flowing brooks and streams, tributaries of the mighty Severn and Wye rivers, powered an array of water-mills in the region. Bran, which is the husks separated from the flour, was a by-product of milling and quarrels were packed into either chests or barrels of bran. It may be that these are the origin of the Christmas bran-tub, since it was chance whether the crossbowmen filled his quiver with high-quality shafts or whether the bran concealed second-rate goods.

Mass-production on such an industrial scale involved the skills of miners, charcoal-burners, smiths, woodmen, fletchers and coopers as well as labour for packing and transport. It is a matter of speculation how many were employed by John de Malemort, but to be ready by July 1277, before Edward I's punitive expedition into Wales, they would have needed to produce approximately 1,500 quarrels per day to meet the March order of 200,000. That is considerably more than the 100–200 quarrels a day that were required when the Malemorts first set up shop for the Crown. Master arrowsmith Hector Cole calculates that the smiths would be able to hammer out a quarrel head in six minutes (private correspondence 2017). Note, however, that would not be every six minutes of an hour – there were forges to maintain and billets of iron to be sorted and forged into blanks before the actual arrowsmithing commenced, as well as some necessary breaks from the relentless pounding. Working in 12-hour shifts, day and night, they could achieve a phenomenal output, but the King's Quarreler required a small army of artisans, probably working with some semblance of an assembly line.

The Forest of Dean was a royal forest and permission had to be granted to fell oaks, beeches, ash and chestnuts. It seems that beech was the timber of choice for quarrel shafts. A royal directive of 1278 instructs the constable of St Briavels: 'Order to cause John de Malemert to have in the forest of Dene two beech-trees for shafts (*flecchas*) for quarrels and two oak-trees to make two chests for the king's use to place the said quarrels in' (CCR Ed I 1278). Edward I's order for 40 crossbows from the sheriff of London was issued on the same day in April 1288 as requisitions for 5,000 quarrels each from the sheriff of Gloucester and the constable of St Briavels. The order continued: 'To the constable of Bristol castle. Order to receive the aforesaid crossbows and quarrels, and to cause them to be carried to Kermerdin [Carmarthen], there to be delivered to the constable of the castle' (CCR Ed I 1288). The date coincides with a great deal of rebuilding at Carmarthen and it may be that the armaments were fresh stock for when it was to be regarrisoned. We cannot know whether or not they augmented an existing arsenal, but it is tempting to speculate that the ratio of consignments represented a typical allocation of quarrels per crossbow. If so, then each crossbow had a supply of 125 quarrels – a resource that would need careful husbandry in the event of a siege.

the fletching. In contrast to the three vanes used on a longbow arrow, a bolt or quarrel only required two. This allowed the bolt to sit flush on the tiller. Materials for bolt fletching included wood, feather, parchment, leather, horn and metal. A total of 2,200 copper-fletched quarrels for crossbows with windlasses were purchased for the English crown's Scottish campaign in 1307 (Liebel 1998: 36). Copper seems a surprisingly expensive choice, but this is by no means the only mention of its use. For the most part it seems that quarrels were ordered and supplied as complete units, with the heads already fitted to the shaft. Even so, Tower Armoury records from 1378, inter alia, refer to 4,760 quarrels with heads and 14,950 quarrels without heads (Richardson 2016: 152).

In 1421, two cases of '*gross traits viretons*' for the great-crossbow called 'Ortie' were inventoried at Blois Castle (Liebel 1998: 36). Ortie belonged to the duke of Orléans. Viretons, also known as vires, were fletched helically. This imparted spin to the flight with the prospect of a stabilizing effect. They seem to have been especially favoured for the large bolts shot from great-crossbows. Late-14th-century accounts for the town arsenal in Bologna record '300 vires with an iron head for great-crossbows partly fletched with horn' (quoted in Liebel 1998: 36). Christine de Pizan itemized 24,000 spinning arrows, 12,000 of them for longer distances (Pizan 1999: 111). Viretons were more expensive. Charles ffoulkes cites an order from 1419 stating the cost at 8s a dozen, compared to 4s a dozen for standard bolts (ffoulkes 1912: 64). A 1543 packing list, that includes some rather dapper hunting gear for Henry VIII, itemized the following, 'Four canvas bags for pheasants. Shoes, black velvet quartered, Spanish leather. 2 crossbows, and 16 forked arrows. 2 vyrall bolts' (LPFD Hen VIII 14). The 16 forked arrows are exactly what we would expect for hunting ammunition, especially when hunting pheasant and a 'vyrall bolt' must surely be the same as a vireton. It is difficult to determine why there were only two out of a provision of 18, but perhaps they were intended for longer-range shots.

RIGHT Replica bolts and quiver by Andreas Bichler. This boarskin quiver has been ornamented with carved bone plates. Wild boar were a prized quarry for the crossbow hunter and the totemic use of the animal's hide for quivers was almost universal. Crossbow bolts were always carried heads-up, affording the most ergonomic movement when taking one and setting it in place. It also allowed the shooter, who may have a variety of heads in his quiver to distinguish them by feel. On other occasions bolts were carried tucked into a belt. This was a practice that had dire consequences for a somewhat boisterous widow by the name of Desiderata. Legal records from Sussex in 1276 recount how she accosted William de Stanegate while he was walking along the road with his crossbow slung over his shoulder. She enquired if he was in pursuit of lawbreakers and bantered that she would be a match for three such as him. Stretching her arm across his neck and sticking her leg behind his, she bowled him over. Stumbling as she did so, she fell upon him and was pierced through the heart by a crossbow bolt tucked into his belt. She died instantly and the verdict was death by misadventure (Bradbury 1985: 78). (Photograph: Andreas Bichler)

FAR RIGHT A common form of crossbow quiver had a distinctive flare at the base. In this example of an original piece, the wooden case was covered with hair-on hide. Although the hair has disappeared with age, the hide can be identified as badger. The two-tone effect of a badger-hide would have given a decorative variation to the more usual boarskin. (Bashford Dean Memorial Collection, Metropolitan Museum of Art, www.metmuseum.org)

THE CROSSBOW AT SEA

Taybughā offered his perspective on the usefulness of the crossbow at sea: 'My own view is that in the manoeuvres of mounted combat, in the desert, and on expeditions the hand bow is a better and more serviceable weapon, whereas in fortresses and sieges, and ships greater power and advantage will be derived from the crossbow' (quoted in Latham & Paterson 1970: 9). In 1241 a law was passed in Denmark (Jutland) that the helmsman on every naval vessel should have, in addition to other weapons, 'a crossbow with three dozen bolts and a man who can shoot with it if he cannot do so himself' (Alm 1994: 23). In the mid-14th century, the accounts of Thomas de Snetesham, Clerk of the (English) King's ships, reveal that despite the popularity of the longbow, crossbows were still considered essential for war at sea. During 1338–39, 256 one-foot crossbows were ordered for the fleet. This compared with 241 longbows. Perhaps more telling was the requirement for 2,496 one-foot quarrels and an astonishing 30,844 two-foot quarrels (Wadge 2007: 159). These last were presumably to provision a large number of great-crossbows that already existed in the fleet. Although longbow-armed infantry would be aboard expeditionary vessels in some numbers, it seems reasonable to suppose that the demand for so many crossbows was to arm the sailors themselves with weapons that they could master with little training.

Arguably, the defining naval engagement of the medieval period was the battle of Sluys (1340). It is covered in some detail in my book *The Longbow* (Loades 2013: 60–62). Even so, it is worth reiterating here that the French had an estimated 20,000 Genoese crossbowmen aboard their ships and that the English force also included large numbers of crossbowmen alongside their more celebrated brothers-in-arms, shooting longbows. The contemporary chronicler Geoffrey le Baker refers to 'an iron shower of bolts from crossbows' during the action (quoted in Bradbury 1985: 102). The cogs of the period, with their augmented defences such as wooden castles, provided ideal conditions for crossbowmen to operate. They could shelter behind stout timbers while loading and then rake the enemy's decks from positions of high advantage. Moreover, as le Baker implies, the fact that a crossbow can be held at full span for a period of time, meant that the crossbowmen could not only time their shots with the swell – they could also shoot in volleys. As well as standard crossbows, most probably those spanned by means of a belt-and-claw, there is evidence for great-crossbows present at Sluys. Liebel cites a reference to a *'ban a tender grosse arbalete'* (a bench for tensioning a great-crossbow) being loaded aboard a ship that set sail for Sluys in 1340. The longer range of the great-crossbow had obvious benefits at sea; not least its capacity for shooting incendiary bolts.

In 1239 the Emperor Frederick II ordered all his ship's captains to have on board 'three good windlass crossbows' (quoted in Liebel 1998: 38); and in about 1400 the admiral of France ordered that should his fleet find themselves in the presence of enemy ships, they should 'greet them with powerful windlass crossbows' (quoted in Liebel 1998: 39). An order from 1441 commands the captains of Genoese ships to carry 28 windlass crossbows on board and 14 windlasses for spanning them (Liebel 1998: 39). This suggests a two-man team, a loader and a shooter, with two crossbows for each spanning device.

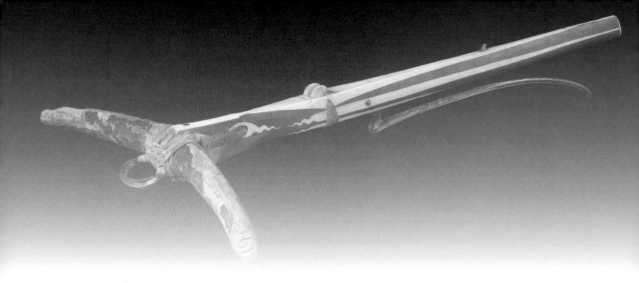

IMPACT
Bolts from the blue

The term 'crossbow' cannot be taken to mean a single weapon type and there can be no blanket assessment of its impact. To quantify the impact of 'a crossbow' would be as meaningless as quantifying the impact of 'a gun', without specifying whether it is a musket, a pistol or a high-powered rifle. Crossbow is a generic, collective term describing a wide variety of weapons with a wide range of capabilities. Each of these has to be assessed according to the precise type and within the context of the armour and battle tactics of the day. Compared to the longbow, little experimental work has been done on crossbows in the modern age and we have to rely more on anecdote.

An entry in *The Warring States Papers* states that

> the hardest bows and most powerful crossbows in the world all come from Han. The bows named 'Xizi', 'Shaofu', 'Shili' and 'Qulai' all have a range of more than six hundred paces. Your Han troops all use their feet to pull their crossbows and when they shoot. Not a shot in one hundred fails in effect: they pierce the chest of any enemy who is far off and the heart of any who is near. (Quoted in Selby 2000: 172)

It was a requirement of Han troops to be able to span a crossbow with a draw-weight of 168lb and it is perhaps reasonable to suppose that this is a likely median draw-weight for the crossbows used by crusading armies; crossbows that were described by Anna Komnene as being spanned in like fashion. In attesting the impact of the crossbow, Komnene does not shrink from hyperbole:

> the missiles do not rebound when they hit a target; in fact they pierce a shield, cut through a heavy iron breastplate and resume their flight

on the far side, so irresistible and violent is the discharge. An arrow of this type has been known to go straight through a bronze statue, and when shot at the wall of a very great town, its point either protruded from the inner side or buried itself in the wall and disappeared altogether … The unfortunate man who is struck by it dies without feeling anything, so strong is the force of the blow. (Komnene 2009: 283)

Although it is plausible that a bolt could embed itself in mud-brick walls or even pierce a hollow bronze statue, it must be remembered that the weapons she is describing are the early wooden-lathed versions of the crossbow, with possibly 100–175lb draw-weight and a power-stroke of 6–7 inches, and that their ability to penetrate armour at anything other than extreme close range seems doubtful. Wooden-lathed crossbows were in exclusive use until about 1200 and remained in common use thereafter, despite the availability of composite bows and subsequently steel bows. To date, however, they have largely been ignored by experimental archaeologists and we do not have data for either their performance or for the maximum poundage achievable in their manufacture.

An illumination from the *Codex Vindobonensis*, Series Nova 2644 (fol. 70v), Tacuinum Sanitatis, housed in the Österreichischen National Bibliotek, Vienna. Although the artist has drawn him standing rather awkwardly, this 14th-century hunter demonstrates aiming with the crossbow by holding the tiller alongside the cheek. He is using a form of forked arrowhead for his avian quarry and has spanned his weapon by means of a belt-and-claw. Notably, the bolt overhangs the bow by a considerable amount and has been fletched with large feathers. It may be that it was designed, like a flu-flu, for short-range shooting and ready retrieval. (Photo by Alinari/Alinari Archives, Florence/Alinari via Getty Images)

AT LONG RANGE

In 1901 Sir Ralph Payne-Gallwey shot a crossbow bolt across the Menai Straits – a distance of around 450 yards (Payne-Gallwey 1981: 14). For this test he used an antique steel lath, which he believed to have been made in Genoa in about 1500. He measured its draw-weight at 1,200lb. The distance he achieved is consistent with the following account from the 16th century. An anonymous correspondent, writing to Lord Walsingham in 1588, during the height of that prolonged summer of naval skirmishing between the English fleet and the Spanish Armada, urged 'the re-introduction of the bow, the crossbow, and the steel bow, as weapons terrible and unused by the enemy. The bow, our natural weapon, good at home but naught abroad; the crossbow flieth far and striketh forcibly, but above all the steel bow, which flieth 20 score [400] yards, and can be discharged twice as fast as the crossbow' (CSPD Eliz I: 520). It is noteworthy that the correspondent emphasizes the distinction between the steel bow and the standard (presumably composite) crossbow. Although steel laths existed from as early as the 15th century, they remained a relatively rare and cutting-edge technology. The sheer quantity of steel-lathed crossbows from later centuries that survive in our museums can give a false impression of the medieval inventory. Although 1,200lb is probably twice the draw-weight that would be possible for the short limbs of a standard composite-lathed crossbow, it is an achievable weight for the longer-limbed great-crossbow with a composite lath.

Great-crossbows

In 2015, Andreas Bichler built and tested a great-crossbow with a draw-weight of 1,276.48lb, comparable to that used by Payne-Gallwey. Bichler's bow is of composite construction, however, based closely on an original in the Schweizerischen Landesmuseum, Zurich. He calculated that it had a draw force of 5,680N at a draw-length (from lath to nut) of 14.7 inches and that the tensioned bow stored nearly 1,277J of energy. Different bolts were used, ranging between 5.4oz and 12.2oz. Measured through a chronograph, these were shot at velocities between 173.60ft/sec and 222.96ft/sec. The 12oz bolt produced a projectile energy of 487.79J,

Reconstruction by Andreas Bichler of a great-crossbow on a windlass-style spanning bench, typical of late 14th- and early 15th-century types. The crossbow is a copy of AG 2570 in the Schweizerischen Landesmuseum and the spanning bench is a copy of one in Castle Sion, Switzerland. Unstrung, the distance between the inner nocks is 59 inches and the length of the tiller is 50 inches. The overall weight is 23lb and the draw-weight is 1,276.48lb! It has been fitted with a 'bastard' or 'false' string in order to bend the lath so that it can receive the standard string. In use, it would either have a prop at the front end of the spanning bench or be removed from the bench and mounted on the castle wall for shooting. When shot it recoils dramatically! (Photograph: Andreas Bichler)

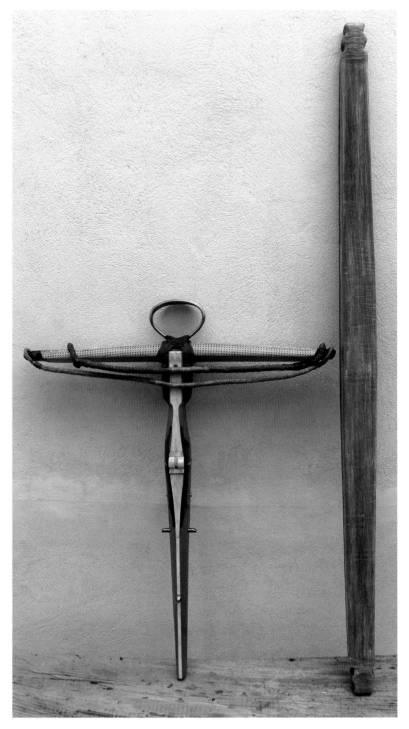

A composite lath for a great-crossbow placed alongside a standard-sized crossbow to show the difference in scale between these two weapons. Both replicas were made by Andreas Bichler. The standard crossbow is a reconstruction of one in the collections of the Landesmuseum, Linz (C 805) and the great-crossbow lath is a reconstruction of an example (AG 2570) in the collections of the Schweizerischen Landesmuseum, Zurich, pictured here before it received its covering of decorated birch bark. (Photograph: Andreas Bichler)

almost equal to the muzzle energy of a 9mm Luger pistol (Sensfelder 2016: 101). At a distance of 26 yards, the quarrel head penetrated a 1.7-inch board of spruce, emerging on the other side by over an inch. The bolt did not pass through. Although not tested for range, it seems likely that Bichler's crossbow would match the distance achieved by Payne-Gallwey.

Crossbows of the same genus may vary considerably in draw-weight and so we should be cautious when ascribing range and impact potential to a particular class of crossbow. Jean Liebel calculates a more modest range, around 275 yards, for great-crossbows, but he makes the point that accuracy may be challenging at long ranges and that long-range shooting was mostly for harassing effect, as when, in 1347, the captain of Bioule ordered his crossbowmen to shoot first with 'the windlass crossbows that shoot further' (quoted in Liebel 1998: 42). As with all military bows, far more important than ultimate range was the potential to deliver force with the strike. Liebel cites an account of the defence of Dijon in 1431 that speaks of great-crossbows capable of 'buckling plate armour' (quoted in Liebel 1998: 41).

AT SHORT RANGE

The crossbow bolt is heavier than a longbow arrow. It is also much shorter and thicker and so is subject to more drag, slowing it down at a faster rate. This loss of velocity translates to a loss in kinetic energy and consequently the force with which the bolt strikes its target. In 2003, tests were conducted at the UK Defence Academy, Shrivenham, as part of a television programme I was presenting about the longbow. We wanted to compare the deceleration of a longbow arrow from a 150lb bow with that of a bolt from a steel-lathed 300lb crossbow, measured with Doppler radar (see Loades 2013: 66). The radar malfunctioned on the day and the results were not conclusive, but the following was observable. The longbow arrow, a heavy livery arrow, began to decelerate early in its flight but continued to fly for around 200 yards. By comparison the crossbow bolt lost very little initial velocity, having a higher-energy launch, but once it started to decelerate, after approximately 60 yards, it did so rapidly, losing any military effectiveness despite continuing to travel another 30 yards or so.

There is an image from the *History of the Northern Peoples* by Olaus Magnus (1553) that shows crossbowmen shooting at cavalry. Lines of arbalists hold the butt of their crossbows at the hip and are shooting at 45 degrees, raining bolts in a parabolic arc (see Alm 1994: 53). They are using a type of bolt, common in Sweden, that has a tanged iron head at least half as long as the overall shaft. Those that have missed their mark create an anti-cavalry spiked field, akin to caltrops. For the most part, however, the crossbow was used as an aimed weapon, holding steady to take out a particular target at relatively close range. In such circumstances, considerations of arrow supply and the optimal range for delivering adequate force with the strike come into play. It was clearly part of the function of the great-crossbow to be able to shoot at greater distances, but for the standard munition, hand-held crossbow, having the capacity to shoot at distance did not mean that long-range shooting was the preferred tactic. Far better to use that power at closer range and to hit the enemy harder.

The heyday of the crossbow as a battlefield arm had passed before the twin technologies of geared cranequins and powerful steel laths transformed the utility weapon of the 12th, 13th and 14th centuries into the potent force it was to become. Until then, the hand-held crossbow was a weapon of only medium power and equal emphasis was placed on speed of loading. The belt-and-claw system remained in general use long after more powerful mechanisms were introduced, which limited the draw-weight a man could manage.

In W.F. Paterson's authoritative study of the crossbow, he states that 'Doubling the draw-weight of a bow, or crossbow,

does not result in doubling the discharge velocity nor the range. At best it will only be increased by one quarter and it is likely to be less. What is of more importance is that a greater draw-weight enables a heavier bolt to be shot without loss of range' (Paterson 1990: 31). Range, to the extent that you can fight an enemy 20–60 yards away, is obviously a key element for projectile weapons. What is most important, however, is that you can strike hard. As discussed in *The Longbow*, the effectiveness of projectile weapons depends not so much on whether armour is penetrated, but rather the level of injury inflicted by blunt force trauma (Loades 2013: 72–74). Similar arguments apply to the crossbow.

With the exception of the specialized longer-range capabilities of the great-crossbow, I would argue that the standard, munition medieval crossbow was intended for relatively close-range use. Early-medieval crossbows were effective battlefield weapons, when used en masse and at short range. It was only during the final decades of the 15th century, when cranequin-spanned crossbows entered general use, that longer-range sniping became a reality. By then, handgonnes had begun to assume the role of close-range artillery and the crossbow, as a military weapon, was already in decline.

A Chinese repeating crossbow, probably dating to the early 20th century. These weapons, essentially unchanged from their original incarnation, remained in use in China until at least the 1950s. This version, having a double magazine and double bolt grooves, shoots two bolts simultaneously. In all other respects it operated identically to the single-magazine weapon illustrated on page 11. (Bath Royal Literary and Scientific Institution Collection)

ARMOUR

Considerations of the crossbow's penetrative power must be evaluated with a full understanding of both the type of armour worn and the type and power of the crossbow in use against it. For a brief survey of some styles of medieval armour see my book *The Longbow* (Loades 2013: 8–14).

During the siege of Acre (1189–91), a crossbow bolt, shot by a Saracen defender, penetrated the three-layered defences of a Frankish sergeant. It went through the mail coif, the mail hauberk beneath it and the padded aketon beneath that. Even so, the man's life was saved by a charm that hung around his neck (Bradbury 1992: 124). Even when a bolt struck home, it did not guarantee certain death. During the siege of Valencia (1238), James the Conqueror was struck in the forehead by a bolt from a crossbow. Although it pierced deeply, he broke off the shaft and witnesses recounted how the blood ran down his face, which he brushed off with a laugh so as not to frighten his army. On returning to his tent, however, his

Armour proofing

It is the primary function of armour to protect its wearer, as best it can, from the weapons of the day. Armour was developed to defend against a variety of attacks, from longbow arrows to lance strikes or sword blows. Nevertheless, there is a parallel graph that may be drawn between the improving metallurgy of plate armour and the increased power of the crossbow, arising from changes in lath technology and spanning devices. There are three elements that offer protection: gauge, shape and hardness. Using thicker-gauge steel added undesirable weight and so, provided that its effectiveness could be demonstrated, lighter armour was preferred. Hardness, created by the alchemical wizardry of the armourer, judging heats and quenches, cannot be seen by the purchaser, however. From the 14th century onwards, it became common practice for armourers to show that their wares were crossbow-proof by shooting a bolt at close range to create a dimple – a proof-mark.

Previously, mail armour was proofed using a sword or axe and by means of a blow, called the *estramaçon*. With the greater threat posed by ever-more-powerful crossbows, however, a crossbow shot became the more usual benchmark of proof. Regulations in 1347 required the wardens of the Heaumers Company of London to oversee proofing, 'also that helmetry and other arms forged by the hammer … shall not from henceforth in any way be offered for sale privily or openly until they have been assayed by the aforesaid wardens and marked with their marks' (quoted in ffoulkes 1912: 65).

In some instances a piece of armour may be marked fully proof; in others merely semi-proof. A clue to the distinction is to be found in the 1448 Statutes of the *Armuriers Fourbisseurs d'Angers*. They state that in order to be fully proofed, an armour must be tested with a windlass crossbow (*arbaleste à tilloles*). Pieces that passed the standard were stamped with two assayer's marks. Semi-proof armours only had to withstand a shot from a belt-and-claw crossbow (*arbaleste à croc*) and were awarded only a single assayer's mark (ffoulkes 1912: 65). Although we get a general idea from this, many variables remain uncertain. At what range were the tests conducted? What type of head was fitted to the bolt? Most importantly, exactly how powerful was the bow? Undoubtedly, a range of different standards existed. An order dating to 1378 in Angers refers specifically to viretons for use when proofing, implying that these helically vaned bolts struck with more force (ffoulkes 1912: 64). A document in the municipal archives of Orléans, dating to 1416, refers to arrows for proofing that have the heads dipped in wax (ffoulkes 1912: 64). It may have been believed that this helped in reducing the effects of deflection, but the merits of this are yet to be tested empirically with modern scientific methods. Moreover, notwithstanding the oversight of the guilds, the proofer was also often the seller and there must have been all manner of ruses to flatter the outcome.

eyes became so swollen that he could not see. Miraculously, James survived the blow, reigning for another 38 years.

Henry VIII's ambassador to the French court, Sir John Wallop, recorded the following incident involving a crossbow in 1543:

> On Saturday afternoon three footmen of the garrison of Arde, returning home from Guisnes, met and quarrelled with two Englishmen coming from Anderne, who, seeing they were two to three and one of the Frenchmen had a crossbow bent, retired; and therewith the Frenchmen cried Tue, Tue, and shot a quarrel at one of them, striking him into the body. He plucked it out and ran furiously to the Frenchmen, of whom he wounded and overcame two with a halbert and the third ran away. That night the Englishman who was shot died, and two days after, the Frenchman that shot him. (LPFD Hen VIII 18)

While the report is vague about precisely where the bolt struck – it seems likely that it was the torso (probably a gut wound, which occasioned the poor fellow's death some hours later) – it is notable that the victim was not only able to pull it out, but to also run and fight with conspicuous valour immediately after he was struck. Of equal note is that his foe was patrolling with his crossbow spanned.

CONCLUSION

Until the advent of viable breech-loading guns in the 19th century, the crossbow remained a superior arm for hunting, notably among European noble elites. Crossbows also continued in service as sporting weapons at the shooting grounds of the European guilds. On the battlefield, the crossbow remained more formidable than gunpowder weapons for some time. As the power of crossbows improved, however, so too did the quality and hardness of armour. For the crossbow to remain relevant on the battlefield, it had to be fielded in its latest manifestation – steel laths, spanned with cranequins or windlasses. Both the steel and the spanning device were an added weight burden for the soldier. Moreover, by 1482 a steel-lathed crossbow cost 6s 8d, which was twice the cost of a handgun (Williams 2003: 49). Furthermore, the cost of gunpowder was falling – and it was significantly less expensive to produce lead balls, which were also recyclable, than it was to manufacture bolts. The crossbow had disappeared from the battlefield by the early 16th century, seeing only occasional use thereafter. Even so, crossbows have continued to be employed by special forces to the present day, used not only as a weapon of stealth but also to deploy zip lines and grappling hooks. One 19th-century example, now in the Imperial War Museum, London, was used to propel hand grenades from the trenches during World War I (1914–18).

Medieval crossbows have, to date, received comparatively little attention from English authors. It is hoped that this brief survey will stimulate more research and motivate the practical experimentation needed to assess more thoroughly the crossbow's military effectiveness, especially for types with wooden and composite laths. During the Middle Ages, crossbows and longbows co-existed; the same men enlisted at times as crossbowmen and at other times as archers. It cannot be said that one weapon was superior to the other; they simply had different, often complementary functions. Archer-historians would do well to embrace the study of both types of bow and to consider them as equal actors on the same stage.

A 16th-century hunting crossbow (A1037) in The Wallace Collection, London. The stock has been elaborately ornamented with incised plates of antler on both the top and bottom. Both sides feature intricate inlaid designs, depicting a hunting scene and augmented with foliage and dot decoration. Note the cords securing the nut. This crossbow has also been fitted with a horn bolt-retaining clip. These clips prevented the bolt from slipping off when angling the bow in either elevation or depression. Holding the bolt in place with a clip was useful for a hunter manoeuvring into position with a spanned bow and also for the mounted crossbowman. Such bolt-retaining clips did not appear until c.1500. Prior to that the arbalist simply placed his thumb, very lightly, over the tail of the bolt to hold it in place while he shot. The steel bow, which is a replacement from the original, has been blackened to discourage rust as well as to remove its glint for hunting. It has been fitted with silk pom-poms. (© The Wallace Collection, London)

BIBLIOGRAPHY

Primary sources

Cal Pat = *Calendar of Patent Rolls, Edward III, 1345–1348.*

CCR Ed I 1277 = 'Close Rolls, Edward I: March 1277', in *Calendar of Close Rolls, Edward I: Vol. 1, 1272–1279*, ed. H.C. Maxwell Lyte (1900), 373–75.

CCR Ed I 1278 = 'Close Rolls, Edward I: January 1278', in *Calendar of Close Rolls, Edward I: Vol. 1, 1272–1279*, ed. H.C. Maxwell Lyte (1900), 435–40.

CCR Ed I 1284 = 'Close Rolls, Edward I: December 1284', in *Calendar of Close Rolls, Edward I: Vol. 2, 1279–1288*, ed. H.C. Maxwell Lyte (1902), 307–09.

CCR Ed I 1288 = 'Close Rolls, Edward I: April 1288', in *Calendar of Close Rolls, Edward I: Vol. 2, 1279–1288*, ed. H.C. Maxwell Lyte (1902), 502–04.

CCR Ed I 1293 = 'Close Rolls, Edward I: October 1293', in *Calendar of Close Rolls, Edward I: Vol. 3, 1288–1296*, ed. H.C. Maxwell Lyte (1904), 303–05.

CCR Ed II = 'Close Rolls, Edward II: August 1326', in *Calendar of Close Rolls, Edward II: Vol. 4, 1323–1327*, ed. H.C. Maxwell Lyte (1898), 638–43.

CCR Ed III = 'Close Rolls, Edward III: September 1328', in *Calendar of Close Rolls, Edward III: Vol. 1, 1327–1330*, ed. H.C. Maxwell Lyte (1896), 413–14.

CCR Rich II = 'Close Rolls, Richard II: July 1390', in *Calendar of Close Rolls, Richard II: Vol. 4, 1389–1392*, ed. H.C. Maxwell Lyte (1922), 274–83.

CSPD Eliz I = *Calendar of State Papers Domestic: Elizabeth, 1581–1590*, ed. Robert Lemon (1865), 520–29.

LPB = 'London Port Book, 1567–8: Nos 500–599 (May–June 1568)', in *The Port and Trade of Early Elizabethan London: Documents*, ed. Brian Dietz (1972), 79–97.

LPFD Hen VIII 3 = *Letters and Papers, Foreign and Domestic, Henry VIII, Vol. 3, 1519–1523*, ed. J.S. Brewer (1867), 345–55.

LPFD Hen VIII 14 = *Letters and Papers, Foreign and Domestic, Henry VIII, Vol. 14 Part 1, January–July 1539*, ed. James Gairdner & R.H. Brodie (1894), 330–48.

LPFD Hen VIII 18 = *Letters and Papers, Foreign and Domestic, Henry VIII, Vol. 18 Part 1, January–July 1543*, ed. James Gairdner & R.H. Brodie (1901), 114–34.

THCN = *An Essay Towards A Topographical History of the County of Norfolk, Vol. 6* (1807).

Published sources

Alm, Joseph, trans. H Bartlett Wells, ed. G.M. Wilson (1994). *European Crossbows: A Survey.* London: The Royal Armouries.

Andrade, Tonio (2016). *The Gunpowder Age.* Princeton, NJ: Princeton University Press.

Bell, Adrian R.; Curry, Anne; King, Andy; Simpkin, David (2013). *The Soldier in Later Medieval England.* Oxford: Oxford University Press.

Blackmore, Howard L. (1971). *Hunting Weapons.* London: Barrie & Jenkins.

Bradbury, Jim (1985). *The Medieval Archer.* Woodbridge: The Boydell Press.

Bradbury, Jim (1992). *The Medieval Siege.* Woodbridge: The Boydell Press.

Breiding, Dirk H. (2013). *A Deadly Art.* New York, NY: The Metropolitan Museum of Art.

Caius, Johannes (2005). *Of Englishe Dogges.* Alcester: Vintage Dog Books. First published in 1576.

Carpenter, D.A. (1996). *The Reign of Henry III.* London: The Hambledon Press.

Crombie, Laura (2016). *Archery and Crossbow Guilds in Medieval Flanders.* Woodbridge: The Boydell Press.

ffoulkes, Charles (1912). *The Armourer and his Craft*. London. Methuen.

Hyland, Anne (1993). *Training the Roman Cavalry*. London: Grange Books.

Komnene, Anna, trans. E.R.A. Sewter (2009). *The Alexiad*. Harmondsworth: Penguin.

Latham, J.D. & Paterson, W.F. (1970). *Saracen Archery*. London: The Holland Press.

Liebel, Jean, trans. Juliet Vale (1998). *Springalds and Great Crossbows*. Leeds: The Royal Armouries.

Loades, Mike (2013). *The Longbow*. Weapon 30. Oxford: Osprey Publishing.

Loades, Mike (2016). *The Composite Bow*. Weapon 43. Oxford: Osprey Publishing.

Paterson, W.F. (1990). *A Guide to the Crossbow*. London: Society of Archer Antiquaries.

Payne-Gallwey, Sir Ralph (1981). *The Crossbow*. London: The Holland Press. Reprint of the 1903 edition.

Pizan, Christine de, trans. Sumner Willard (1999). *The Book of Deeds of Arms and of Chivalry*. University Park, PA: Penn State University Press.

Powicke, F.M (1960). *The Loss of Normandy 1189–1204*. Manchester: Manchester University Press.

Powicke, Michael (1962). *Military Obligation in Medieval England*. Oxford: Oxford University Press.

Richardson, Thom (2016). *The Tower Armoury in the Fourteenth Century*. Leeds: The Royal Armouries.

Selby, Stephen (2000). *Chinese Archery*. Hong Kong: Hong Kong University Press.

Selby, Stephen, (2003). *Archery Traditions of Asia*. Hong Kong: Hong Kong Museum of Coastal Defence.

Sensfelder, Jens (2016). *Jahrblatt der Interessengemeinschaft Historische Armbrust*. Norderstedt: Books on Demand.

Smail, R.C. (1995). *Crusading Warfare 1097–1193*. Cambridge: Cambridge University Press.

Smythe, Sir John (1964). *Certain Discourses Military*. Washington, DC: Folger Shakespeare Library. Originally published in 1590.

Storey, Randall (1998). 'The Tower of London and the garderobe armorum', in *Royal Armouries Yearbook 3*. Leeds: The Royal Armouries.

Strickland, Matthew & Hardy, Robert (2005). *The Great Warbow*. Stroud: Sutton Publishing.

Turnbull, Stephen (2001). *Siege Weapons of the Far East (1)*. New Vanguard 43. Oxford: Osprey Publishing.

Tyerman, Christopher (1988). *England and the Crusades*. Chicago, IL: University of Chicago Press.

Wadge, Richard (2007). *Arrowstorm*. Stroud: The History Press.

Wendover, Roger of, trans. J.A. Giles (1849). *Flores Historiarum*. London: H.G. Bohn.

Williams, Alan (2003). *The Knight and the Blast Furnace*. Leiden: Brill.

Wilson, Guy M. (2007). 'What's in a Name? One-Foot and Two-Foot Crossbows', in Robert D. Smith, ed., *ICOMAM 50: Papers on Arms and Military History 1957–2007*. Leeds: ICOMAM: pp. 300–25.

INDEX